KT-364-930

Contents

Introduction

MONEY ISSUES is Volume 322 in the **ISSUES** series. The aim of the series is to offer current, diverse information about important issues in our world, from a UK perspective.

ABOUT MONEY ISSUES

The landscape of money and finances in the UK, and globally, is a fast changing topic. This book explores the issues of family finances, credit, loans and savings. It also looks at developments like bitcoin and the rise of cryptocurrencies. In addition to this, it considers trends such as mobile wallets and moving towards a cashless economy.

The information inside comes from a variety of sources, including newspapers, magazines, government reports and charity groups; providing different perspectives on challenging topics. At the end of the book is a selection of activities that will encourage interaction, literacy, critical thinking and independent research. Content is accessible and engaging, tailored primarily towards the 14 to 18 age group.

OUR SOURCES

Titles in the **ISSUES** series are designed to function as educational resource books, providing a balanced overview of a specific subject.

The information in our books is comprised of facts, articles and opinions from many different sources, including:

⇨ Newspaper reports and opinion pieces

⇨ Website factsheets

⇨ Magazine and journal articles

⇨ Statistics and surveys

⇨ Government reports

⇨ Literature from special interest groups.

A NOTE ON CRITICAL EVALUATION

Because the information reprinted here is from a number of different sources, readers should bear in mind the origin of the text and whether the source is likely to have a particular bias when presenting information (or when conducting their research). It is hoped that, as you read about the many aspects of the issues explored in this book, you will critically evaluate the information presented.

It is important that you decide whether you are being presented with facts or opinions. Does the writer give a biased or unbiased report? If an opinion is being expressed, do you agree with the writer? Is there potential bias to the 'facts' or statistics behind an article?

ASSIGNMENTS

In the back of this book, you will find a selection of assignments designed to help you engage with the articles you have been reading and to explore your own opinions. Some tasks will take longer than others and there is a mixture of design, writing and research-based activities that you can complete alone or in a group.

FURTHER RESEARCH

At the end of each article we have listed its source and a website that you can visit if you would like to conduct your own research. Please remember to critically evaluate any sources that you consult and consider whether the information you are viewing is accurate and unbiased.

Useful weblinks

www.bangor.ac.uk

www.blog.themoneyshed.co.uk

www.blog.lemonademoney.com

www.theconversation.co.uk

www.demos.co.uk

www.financialinclusioncommission. org.uk

www.theguardian.com

www.hindustantimes.com

www.huffingtonpost.co.uk

www.ibtimes.com

www.imf.org

www.independent.co.uk

www.intelligentenvironments

www.moneyadviceservice.org.uk

www.ons.gov.uk

www.opinium.co.uk

www.royallondon.com

www.santander.co.uk

www.stepchange.org

www.thetelegraph.co.uk

www.toynbeehall.org.uk

www.youngmoneyblog.co.uk

www.yourmoney.com

www.yougov.co.uk

Independence Educational Publishers

First published by Independence Educational Publishers

The Studio, High Green

Great Shelford

Cambridge CB22 5EG

England

© Independence 2017

Copyright

Photocopy licence

ISBN-13: 978 1 86168 772 2

Printed in Great Britain

Zenith Print Group

Family spending in the UK: financial year ending March 2016

An insight into the spending habits of UK households, broken down by household characteristics and types of spending.

Main points

Average weekly household spending remained level at £528.90 in the financial year ending 2016, coinciding with a slowdown in consumer confidence.

Low-income households continued to spend a higher proportion of their expenditure on food and energy when compared with households with a higher income.

UK households spent more than £45.00 a week on restaurants and hotels for the first time in five years.

Average weekly spending on alcohol, tobacco and narcotics fell below £12.00 for the first time.

Over half of money spent on communication was spent on a mobile phone-related cost.

Things you need to know about this release

Figures in this bulletin are averaged across all UK households, unless stated otherwise.

This bulletin uses the mean when referring to averages. Therefore, total average weekly household expenditure is equal to the total weekly expenditure of households divided by the number of households.

This bulletin compares spending over time in two different ways, where figures are either adjusted for inflation or not adjusted for inflation. Where figures are not adjusted for inflation, differences in spending could be because of differences in price level between the years. When comparing spending that has been adjusted for inflation, differences in price between years are not a legitimate reason for differences in spending, as this has already been taken into account. Where possible, we adjust for inflation when comparing levels of spending over time. However, for more detailed expenditure items this is not possible and we therefore compare unadjusted figures. Please see the Quality and methodology section on the website for more information on comparisons over time.

Changes and differences said to be statistically significant are significant at the 95% confidence level, unless stated otherwise.

This bulletin considers expenditure by UK constituent country and English region. We combine three years of data when presenting spending broken down by country and region in order to improve the robustness of results.

Spending is presented using classification of individual consumption by purpose (COICOP) categories, unless otherwise stated. COICOP is an internationally recognised classification system consistent with that used by UK National Accounts. It does not include all types of payments; for example, capital mortgage repayments are excluded. Due to high interest in this topic, this bulletin also considers housing costs outside the COICOP classification system. Further information on COICOP can be found on the United Nations Statistics Division website.

We use equivalised disposable income decile groups when looking at expenditure and income together. Disposable income is defined as gross weekly cash income less the statutory deductions and payments of Income Tax and National Insurance contributions. It is used alongside

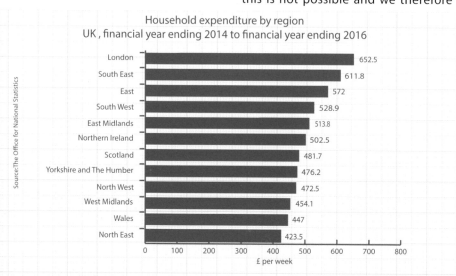

Household expenditure by region
UK , financial year ending 2014 to financial year ending 2016

Region	£ per week
London	652.5
South East	611.8
East	572
South West	528.9
East Midlands	513.8
Northern Ireland	502.5
Scotland	481.7
Yorkshire and The Humber	476.2
North West	472.5
West Midlands	454.1
Wales	447
North East	423.5

Source: The Office for National Statistics

expenditure as it is the amount households have available to spend or save. Equivalisation takes into account that households with many members are likely to need a higher income to achieve the same standard of living as households with fewer members. Please see the Quality and methodology section on the website for more information on equivalisation. For ownership of durable goods, gross income decile groups are used. The standard concept of gross income is gross weekly cash income current at the time of interview; that is, before the deduction of Income Tax actually paid, National Insurance contributions and other deductions at source.

Results presented in this bulletin cover the financial year ending 2016 (2015/16); that is, April 2015 to March 2016. The move to financial year comes following user demand. Financial year ending 2015 (2014/15) tables are also available to provide comparability.

Family Spending has been designated by the UK Statistics Authority as National Statistics, in accordance with the Statistics and Registration Service Act 2007 and signifying compliance with the Code of Practice for Official Statistics

Total spending remained unchanged when compared with a year ago

Total average weekly household expenditure remained level at £528.90 in the financial year ending 2016 (2015/16) when compared with the same period a year ago.

16 February 2017

⇨ The above information was reprinted with kind permission from The Office for National Statistics. Please visit www.ons. gov.uk for further information.

© Crown copyright 2017

Families spend a third of their income on childcare – UK most expensive in the world

There are lots of great things about living in the UK… roast dinners, afternoon tea and our polite and friendly attitude. However it seems that our childcare costs are letting the side down! It has been revealed that we have the most expensive childcare in the world, according to a study by the Organisation for Economic Cooperation and Development (OECD).

'A full-time nursery place for a child under two costs an eye-watering £222 a week, meaning working families are now spending £11,300 a year on average on childcare. This increases to £15,700 in London (gulp!).

Shockingly, this is more than three times the cost of childcare in France and Germany, with parents in the UK spending more than a third of their income on nurseries and childminders.

It is probably no surprise that childcare costs tend to be higher in English-speaking countries, with European countries falling lower on the list as they provide much more funding for childcare to allow mothers to continue to work.

There are plans to increase the amount of free childcare in the UK to 30 hours a week for children aged three and four in 2017. But this is dependant on family income levels and there is still no extra help for families who have children under three.

When you have young children, this is potentially the time in your life where your money is stretched to its absolute maximum. As boring as it may be, it is a time where you need to keep a close eye on your finances and doing a monthly or weekly budget can help.

October 2016

⇨ The above information is reprinted with kind permission from Lemonade Money Blog. Please visit www.blog.lemonademoney.com for further information.

© 2017 Lemonade Money Blog

'Bank of Mum and Dad' to hand over £6.5 Billion to children for property in 2017, report claims

'What about those without an inheritance or wealthy parents?'

By Jasmine Gray

News that the 'Bank of Mum and Dad' will pump £6.5 billion into property transactions this year has reignited debate over Britain's "broken" housing market.

Research from Legal & General and Cebr showed that parents will be involved in 26% of all property transactions in 2017, contributing towards more than 298,000 mortgages and helping to purchase homes worth £75 billion.

The findings put the 'Bank of Mum and Dad' on par with the Yorkshire Building Society, the ninth largest mortgage lender in the UK, the Press Association reported.

But they have infuriated many people, with some criticising the current system for barring social mobility.

Responding to the report, Labour MP David Lammy said the "broken, deeply unfair housing market" was "entrenching inequality".

The former higher education minister tweeted: "What about those without an inheritance or without wealthy parents?"

"Concept of 'affordable' homes has lost all meaning across the country"

According to the report, millennials will be the biggest recipients of the cash, with 79% of the money going to people under 30.

But dozens of young people pointed out on social media today that their parents can't afford to give them money for a deposit.

"Bank of Mum and Dad really annoys me. Some of us don't have that option, at all! We have to work harder and longer. We know real value."

Helen Lambert (@Heeerins)

"I cannot rely on the Bank of Mum and Dad, due to being an orphan and all. Guess I shall just resign myself to mediocre living standards."

Jay Thomas @ThisJayThomas

"Closest I have to a Bank of Mum and Dad is the huge jar of pennies my Dad seems to be keeping to use as a weapon in the revolution."

Rebecca Winson @rebeccawinson

'Got nowt from the bank of mum and dad. Only thing my parents gave me is an inability to throw away a carrier bag in case it might be useful.'

joe x @mutablejoe

"Hi. I'm 30 and have a decent job, but priced out of where I live. I'd like to make a withdrawal from the Bank of Mum and Dad please."

pic.twitter.com/tQtYvR48hK
— Vonny Moyes (@vonny_bravo)

"Like many my age, I had access to the bank of Mum and Dad. Sadly, all I got were some pens they'd forgotten to chain down."

Oonagh @Okeating

Legal & General chief executive Nigel Wilson said: "The Bank of Mum and Dad continues to grow in importance in helping young people take their early steps on to the housing ladder.

"The inter-generational inequality that creates the demand for Bank of Mum and Dad funding continues to widen – younger people today don't have the same opportunities that the baby-boomers had, including affordable housing, defined benefit pensions and free university education.

"Parents want to help their kids get on in life, and the Bank of Mum and Dad is a testament to their generosity, but it is also a symptom of our broken housing market."

He said the UK was experiencing a "supply-side crisis" in housing, adding: "We need to build more homes for the young, old and families alike – more quickly and cost effectively."

2 May 2017

⇨ The above information is reprinted with kind permission from Huffington Post. Please visit www.huffingtonpost.co.uk for further information.

Pocket money

The ins and outs of pocket money.

By Maria Stonehouse

The majority (60%) of parents giving their children pocket money do so once a week, while one in six (12%) give their children pocket money every day. The average value of pocket money that parents give their children on a weekly basis is £11.

'Almost two-thirds (63%) of parents expect pocket money to be spent on sweets and chocolate, however, half (49%) expect their children to buy DVDs and CDs with their pocket money, 45% expect tickets (for the cinema, theatre or concert) to be bought and 44% expect their children to buy video games'

Pocket money and gender: a gender pay gap?

Unsurprisingly, factors such as the age of a child has an effect on how much pocket money they are given. However, findings also suggest that this is also the case for gender. For boys, the average amount of pocket money given on a weekly basis is £11.47. For girls, this is £10.67, a reduction of 80p.

Controlling and determining the amount of pocket money given

Although the majority of parents give pocket money to their children, there are different parenting styles with regards to how this is managed. A quarter (23%) of parents say they always control what their children spend their pocket money on. A fifth (18%) never interfere with how their children use theirs, and a fifth (21%) encourage their children to save all the pocket money they are given.

Other factors that influence how much pocket money parents give to their children are:

⇨ The cost of items their children want (39%)

⇨ Recent behaviour (37%)

⇨ School grades (30%).

Although there are different parenting styles to teaching children the value of money, over three in five (65%) of all parents surveyed agree that pocket money teaches children this value. Other top skills that parents think giving pocket money enables are the ability to budget and plan their spending (60% agree) and the ability to save money (59%).

Opinium Research carried out an online survey of 1,057 UK parents of children aged 11 to 18 years old from the 20 to 23 October 2015. The value for pocket money given was derived from online surveys (also amongst parents aged 11 to 18 years old), which were carried out throughout November 2015.

7 December 2015

The startling statistics on pocket money: how much should your children get?

Pocket money is a huge issue for parents. When should it start? How much should you give? Should it be linked to chores or jobs? Here are some facts and figures to help you decide.

"Parents in the UK are more generous than their European counterparts early on, but end up paying their teenage children well below the European average"

Under-fives: Children under the age of five receive £2 a week in the UK, compared with 80p in Spain, 40p in The Netherlands and £1.60 in France. The Italians are more indulgent, at £4.

5–10: Between five and ten, children in the UK receive £5 a week – more than in Europe where Italian, Spanish and French parents give their children an average £4 per week.

10–15: Between the ages of ten and 15, pocket money in the UK remains frozen at £5 a week, while in Italy, France, Spain, Germany and Luxembourg it rises to £8.

15 up: From age 15 onwards UK parents give an average of £9.50 a week, compared with £28 a week in Austria and £40 in Luxembourg. Belgium, Italy, France and Germany give £24. Only parents in Poland, Romania and the Czech Republic dole out less each week than those in the UK – £9.40, £8.80 and £8.60, respectively.

The gender pay gap starts early

For UK boys, the average amount of pocket money given on a weekly basis is £11.47. Girls get 80p less, at £10.67.

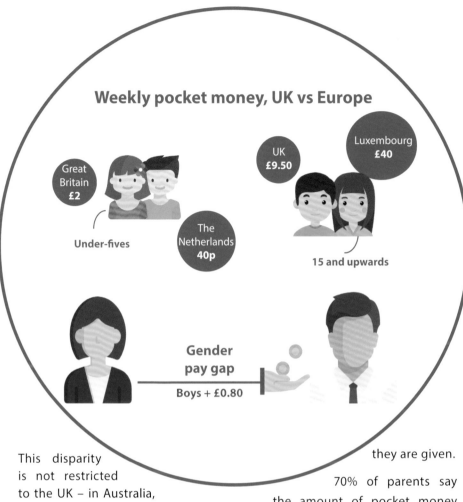

Weekly pocket money, UK vs Europe

Great Britain £2 · Under-fives

The Netherlands 40p

UK £9.50 · Luxembourg £40 · 15 and upwards

Gender pay gap
Boys + £0.80

This disparity is not restricted to the UK – in Australia, new research by The Australian Council of Trade Unions shows girls get 11% less pocket money than boys, and female university graduates get 18% less than men.

Pocket money outstrips pay rises

From the age of 11, the average amount of pocket money rises by 18% per year – or £1.78.

Do parents have a say in how pocket money is earned and spent?

23% of parents say they always control what their children spend their pocket money on, while 18% never interfere. 21% encourage their children to save all the pocket money they are given.

70% of parents say the amount of pocket money given is dependent on chores, such as helping to tidy the house (35%), washing the car (29%) and taking out the rubbish (27%).

Other parents will alter the amount given in pocket money depending on the cost of items their children want (39%); recent behaviour (37%); and school grades (30%).

Hard cash or digital payments?

Research commissioned by financial technology firm Intelligent Environments found that 80% of parents introduced their children to digital money management from a young age.

Creating savings habits for life

A survey from ING bank found that 55% of people who received pocket money when they were children regularly added to their savings as adults, compared with 45% who didn't.

Seven in ten parents of children aged five to 18 say they give their eldest child pocket money (70%). Half say the main reason for this is to help their child learn about and manage money independently (51%).

Talking to children about money

UK parents can do better when it comes to educating their children about money. Only half (52%) say they discuss money matters regularly with their children. The average age at which they talk to them about saving is nine, yet the average age at which children start to receive pocket money is eight, and they begin to form money habits by age seven.

15 July 2016

⇨ The above information is reprinted with kind permission from *The Guardian*. Please visit www.theguardian.com for further information.

© 2017 Guardian News and Media Limited

Pocket money – why it needs to survive in the digital age

By Harry Wallop

As a survey suggests pocket money is declining, we look at how the tradition can flourish in an increasingly cashless society

"Can I have £5.50," asks Celia, my seven-year-old.

"Why?"

"I really want to buy this doll," she says, pointing to a slightly damaged and distinctly terrifying porcelain figure dressed in Victorian garb. We spent part of half-term in Suffolk, home to many wonderful sights, not least Clare Antiques, four-floors of vintage clothing, dusty armoury and disturbing dolls. The kids loved it.

"Use your pocket money," I say.

"But, you don't give me any," she answers.

She is correct. I can never remember which of my four children gets pocket money, who gets "holiday money", and who just accumulates cash from overgenerous relations at Christmas in mythical escrow accounts.

We are not the only family to find pocket money a source of mild anxiety: what age do you start giving? How much to pay? Should it be given in return for doing chores, or handed over strings-free? But this generation could be the last to know the thrill and discipline of waiting for a regular weekly amount from their parents.

Figures released by Halifax, which has conducted an annual pocket money survey since 1987, suggests the average amount children receive (aged between eight and 15) fell last year, from £6.35 a week to £6.20. This is the second consecutive year the amount has fallen. Indeed, the amounts are down considerably from the high it reached pre-recession in 2005, when it hit £8.37.

Some have welcomed the idea that children are finally feeling the effects of austerity, like the rest of us. Jasmine Birtles, who runs the personal finance website Moneymagpie, says: "I am rather pleased the pocket money index has fallen. For many years it significantly outperformed inflation, and outperformed everything, even after the crash in 2008. And I felt it was wrong that it was so high. It seemed to be fuelled a bit by guilt, with divorced parents buying off their children. I hope a bit of reality has finally been injected into pocket money."

But the figures tell another, possibly worrying story. Not only has the average amount fallen among those who receive pocket money, but the proportion of children receiving a weekly sum has also decreased – down from 82 per cent to 78 per cent.

Sarah Boratero, a mother-of-four in Somerset who gives £5 a week to her nine-year-old daughter, is a firm fan of pocket money. "A lot of her friends have no idea of the value of the money," she says. "They don't even have a concept of spending, because everything they ask for is bought for them."

Spending, of course, has become an even more complex phenomenon in the digital age. Even preschool children realise money can be spent not just in a toy shop, but also online, with the likes of Moshi Monsters or Club Penguin requiring membership fees if you want to play the best games.

"I do think it is much harder for parents now," says Ian Williams, who works for Thinkmoney, which offers basic bank accounts to those who struggle to keep to a budget. "Children can come down for an evening meal from their bedroom, having been spending away merrily online."

Now that nearly all secondary school pupils have their own mobile phone, as well as digital devices such as a tablet on which to do their school work, many parents end up paying monthly subscription fees on multiple devices.

Some argue, however, that old-fashioned pocket money is more important than ever. Last week, figures from the Payments Council showed that the number of cashless transactions have overtaken the use of physical money for the first time, as more shops accept 'contactless' cards, with which you can pay for a £2 coffee or sandwich at the tap of a reader.

Tom Sefton, economic adviser at the Church of England, says: "We think it is very important that children do not skip straight to a cashless society. For many children, transactions done on a card or over the Internet does not feel particularly real."

The Church, indeed, believes financial education is crucial for families who want to avoid sinking into debt and relying on payday lenders, against whom it fought a concerted (and controversial) campaign. Indeed, it has announced it will pilot savings clubs for children in primary schools in the next academic year, in partnership with credit unions. "Children must learn the importance of saving from an early age," says Sefton. "We're talking small amounts, but studies show that if children handle their own money, rather than parents saving it on their behalf, they will develop good financial habits."

A Europe-wide survey from ING, the bank, found that those who received pocket money as children were more likely as adults to contribute to a savings account, and less likely to be overdrawn.

Pocket money, then, is a good thing – whether it is given as a reward for completing chores or just handed over as a regular weekly payment. "As long as the rules of engagement are clear, children will understand," says Birtles.

It would be easy to feel glum about the slow demise of pocket money, but it is far from dead – not least evidenced by the boom in pocket-money toys. This market was given enormous boost by the decision of Lego, in 2010, to start selling its mini-figures – called "minifigs" by children – in individual packs, costing £2. Cheap and collectable, they became a playground craze.

The next year, they were Britain's most popular toy by a country mile, and since then many companies have attempted to cash in on this price-point, from Playmobil to loom bands. Last year, helped by the Panini World Cup stickers, the toy market increased by 4 per cent, but those products under £3 jumped by 19 per cent, according to NPD, which monitors

the toy market. Children are still very much spending money.

Also, in the last two years, two major apps have been developed to take advantage of the increasing move from notes and coins to digital spending. Called Osper and goHenry, they are, in effect, very basic bank online accounts (without any overdraft facility) for children aged eight and upwards.

Both work by parents transferring real money, via their own bank account or debit card, to a children's account. In both cases, children are given prepaid cards that they can use to buy products on the high street or online. GoHenry has teamed up with Visa, while Osper's partner is MasterCard.

Williams says: "I know many parents are appalled at the idea of kids being mugged or marched off the cashpoint, but where I grew up, kids were mugged for their pocket money. Intellectually, it is no different."

And though it is a modern twist, it is very similar to the Post Office account I remember fondly from my childhood (though perhaps my memories may have coloured by the spike in interest rates in the early 1980s, which saw my meagre Christmas money swell very rapidly).

Over the last year, I have started to use goHenry for my two eldest boys, aged nine and 12. And it has mostly been a big success, apart from rather annoyingly large operating fees (£1.97 per child per month – a small amount, but a large percentage in pocket money terms). While it means the boys don't get the experience of handling real cash, it does allow them to see – on their phones or tablets – exactly what they have spent, and what they have left in their account. I can also restrict which shops or websites in which they spend their money, and can set limits as to how much they can spend in a single transaction.

It has also, crucially, stopped arguments about what they have to spend – and whether I have actually handed over the pocket money. It might even give them a harsh lesson in the perils of deflation.

7 December 2015

⇨ The above information is reprinted with kind permission from The Telegraph News and Media. Please visit www.thetelegraph.co.uk for further information.

The ATM at 50: how a hole in the wall changed the world

By Bernardo Batiz-Lazo

Next time you withdraw money from a hole in the wall, consider singing a rendition of happy birthday. For on 27 June, the Automated Teller Machine (or ATM) celebrates its half-century. 50 years ago, the first cash machine was put to work at the Enfield branch of Barclays Bank in London. Two days later, a Swedish device known as the Bankomat was in operation in Uppsala. And a couple of weeks after that, another one built by Chubb and Smith Industries was inaugurated in London by Westminster Bank (today part of RBS Group).

These events fired the starting gun for today's self-service banking culture – long before the widespread acceptance of debit and credit cards. The success of the cash machine enabled people to make impromptu purchases, spend more money on weekend and evening leisure, and demand banking services when and where they wanted them. The infrastructure, systems and knowledge they spawned also enabled bankers to offer their customers point of sale terminals, and telephone and Internet banking.

There was substantial media attention when these "robot cashiers" were launched. Banks promised their customers that the cash machine would liberate them from the shackles of business hours and banking at a single branch. But customers had to learn how to use – and remember – a PIN, perform a self-service transaction and trust a machine with their money.

People take these things for granted today, but when cash machines first appeared many had never before been in contact with advanced electronics.

"And the system was far from perfect. Despite widespread demand, only bank customers considered to have 'better credit' were offered the service. The early machines were also clunky, heavy (and dangerous) to move, insecure, unreliable and seldom conveniently located"

"Indeed, unlike today's machines, the first ATMs could do only one thing:

dispense a fixed amount of cash when activated by a paper token or bespoke plastic card issued to customers at retail branches during business hours. Once used, tokens would be stored by the machine so that branch staff could retrieve them and debit the appropriate accounts. The plastic cards, meanwhile, would have to be sent back to the customer by post. Needless to say, it took banks and technology companies years to agree common standards and finally deliver on their promise of 24/7 access to cash'

The globalisation effect

Estimates by RBR London concur with my research, suggesting that by 1970, there were still fewer than 1,500 of the machines around the world, concentrated in Europe, North America and Japan. But there were 40,000 by 1980 and a million by 2000.

"It's a good time to consider what the history of cash dispensers can teach us. The ATM was not the result of a eureka moment of a single middle-aged man in a bath or garage, but from active collaboration between various groups of bankers and engineers to solve the significant challenges of a changing world. It took two decades for the ATM to mature and gain widespread, worldwide acceptance, but today there are 3.5 million ATMs with another 500,000 expected by 2020"

A number of factors made this ATM explosion possible. First, sharing locations created more transaction volume at individual ATMs. This gave

incentives for small and medium-sized financial institutions to invest in this technology. At one point, for instance, there were some 200 shared ATM networks in the US and 80 shared networks in Japan.

They also became more popular once banks digitised their records, allowing the machines to perform a host of other tasks, such as bank transfers, balance requests and bill payments. Over the last five decades, a huge number of people have made the shift away from the cash economy and into the banking system. Consequently, ATMs became a key way of avoiding congestion at branches.

ATM design began to accommodate people with visual and mobility disabilities, too. And in recent decades, many countries have allowed non-bank companies, known as Independent ATM Deployers (IAD) to operate machines. The IAD were key to populating non-bank locations such as corner shops, petrol stations and casinos.

Indeed, while a large bank in the UK might own 4,000 devices and one in the US as many as 12,000, Cardtronics, the largest IAD, manages a fleet of 230,000 ATMs in 11 countries.

Bank to the future

The ATM has remained a relevant and convenient self-service channel for the last half century – and its history is one of invention and re-invention, evolution rather than revolution.

Self-service banking and ATMs continue to evolve. Instead of PIN authentication, some ATMS now use "tap and go" contactless payment technology using bank cards and mobile phones. Meanwhile, ATMs in Poland and Japan have used biometric recognition, which can identify a customer's iris, fingerprint or voice, for some time, while banks in other countries are considering them.

Research I am currently undertaking suggests that ATMs may have reached

saturation point in some Western countries. However, research by the ATM Industry Association suggests there is strong demand for them in China, India and the Middle East. In fact, while in the West people tend to use them for three self-service functions (cash withdrawal, balance enquiries, and purchasing mobile phone airtime), Chinese consumers regularly use them for as many as 100 different tasks.

Taken for granted?

Interestingly, people in most urban areas around the world tend to interact with the same five ATMs. But they shouldn't be taken for granted. In many countries in Africa, Asia and South America, they offer services to millions of people otherwise excluded from the banking sector.

In most developed countries, meanwhile, the retail branch and the ATM are the only two channels over which financial institutions have 100% control. This is important when you need to verify the authenticity of your customer. Banks do not control the make and model of their customers' smart phones, tablets or personal computers, which are vulnerable to hacking and fraud. While ATMs are targeted by thieves, mass cybernetic attacks on them have yet to materialise.

"I am often asked whether the advent of a cashless, digital economy heralds the end of the ATM. My response is that while the world might do away with cash and call ATMs something else, the revolution of automated self-service banking that began 50 years ago is here to stay."

26 June 2017

⇨ The above information is reprinted with kind permission from *The Conversation*. Please visit www.theconversation for further information.

Millions of Brits have no savings

⇨ Brits save an average £150 each month – a collective £81.8 billion a year

⇨ But a fifth have no savings at all and 18 per cent save £50 or less

⇨ 53% wish they had received more money advice at a younger age as 78% believe being "good with money" is a learned behaviour

New analysis from Santander UK reveals that 10.3 million Brits (20 per cent) have no savings, leaving them exposed to unexpected expenditure. Although the average Brit saves £150 per month, a collective £81.8 billion a year, almost a fifth (18 per cent) save £50 or less.

The study, which investigates the savings habits of the nation, reveals that 52 per cent of people wish they could save more, on average an additional £388 each month. The most popular way to put money aside is in a savings account (53 per cent) followed by a Cash ISA (27 per cent). However, many Brits overlook investing as a way to manage their money with only one in ten (12 per cent) saying they invest and utilise Stocks and Shares ISAs.

In fact, half of Brits (53 per cent) wish they had received more money advice at a younger age, rising to two-thirds (66 per cent) for those aged 18 to 34, and decreasing to 42 per cent for those aged 55 and over. A quarter of UK adults (26 per cent) wish they had been taught more about investments and 21 per cent about budgeting, while almost one in five (19 per cent) wish they had received more advice about the different savings options available to them.

Helen Bierton, Head of Savings at Santander, said: "Our research shows that although many of us are saving, there is still a significant number who have no savings to fall back on or are not aware of all the options available. Developing a savings habit – no matter how small – is so important as it not only provides a safety net but is a way of providing for your future, and those of your loved ones.

"Santander offers a range of savings products with different options to suit individual customer needs and to help people achieve their savings goals, including both Cash and Stocks and Shares ISAs. For those considering investments, we recently launched our Investment Hub to make investing more accessible with investments from as little as £20 a month."

The findings also highlight that more than three quarters of UK adults (78 per cent) believe that being "good with money" is a learned behaviour that anyone can pick up with practice. In comparison, only 13 per cent believe that being either good or bad with money comes naturally and is a behaviour that cannot be learned or influenced in any way.

When asked who had been the biggest influencer on their money and savings behaviour, over two fifths (43 per cent) revealed their parents had been their example to follow, compared to one in ten (11 per cent) who mentioned their partner as their biggest influence.

Dr Sam Wass, Channel 4 psychologist and research scientist at the University of East London, commented: "There are lots of factors that affect who saves up their money and who doesn't – such as our willpower, and how much we value our long-term happiness over a more immediate, short-term reward. The research shows that most people agree being good with money is a learned skill and there are various techniques we can use to help us to improve our willpower and our organisational skills. It's never too late to start!"

Almost two-thirds of Brits (64 per cent) say that their friends or family would describe them as being "good with money". Of these, almost three quarters (73 per cent) pay all their bills on time, half (50 per cent) seek out promotional offers rather than paying full price, 44 per cent keep an eye on their bills to see if they could be getting a better deal and 38 per cent pay off their full credit card balance at the end of each month. However, not everyone is so money savvy, of those who claim they are "bad with money", 59 per cent say they run out of spending money before payday and 30 per cent have a lump sum of debt sitting in their account that doesn't get paid off.

Most people say they are saving to increase their buffer pot (44 per cent) followed by a holiday (34 per cent) and to pay unexpected bills (26 per cent). A fifth (22 per cent) aim to top up their retirement pots and a further 14 per cent are saving for a home.

For more information on Santander's savings products please visit: www.santander.co.uk/savings.

15 March 2017

⇨ The above information is reprinted with kind permission from Santander UK. Please visit www.santander.co.uk for further information

New report solves the savings puzzle for low-income households

A new report published today by the Financial Health Exchange, within Toynbee Hall, supported by J.P. Morgan, finds that informal savings techniques help low income households to be financially resilient.

Savings for the Future; Solving the savings puzzle for low-income households, finds evidence for a variety of personal motivations that help low income households to put away small amounts of money, including for rewards like family treats and holidays. Also for less obvious reasons such as having pride in being able to have a savings fund at all, particularly for people who have not always been able to save.

This research helps to dispel the myth that low income households do not have savings methods or personal techniques for financial resilience, but find that these methods are often overpowered by other external pressures like low wages or the rising cost of living.

The research shows that there are six types of saver:

⇨ The spend-saver: saving through careful spending.

⇨ The reward-treat saver: short term savers who hold money back to spend on a treat.

⇨ Safety net saver: short-medium term savers who are saving to avoid unexpected expenses.

⇨ Life goal saver: savers, medium to long term, whose goal is a stress-free pension age, or big purchases like a house or car.

⇨ 'Saving just to save' saver: savers who are simply rewarded and proud to be able to save, typically those who have previously found it difficult to save money.

⇨ Passive saver: those people – rare among low income households – who have savings but are not actively taking steps to save money. This can often be where an income more than meets the needs of an individual's expenditure, or after a windfall like a lottery win.

"This report has created a brand new typology of low income savers, calls for the development of new partnerships between debt advice agencies, financial service providers and FinTech start-ups, and the design of a brand new financial support programme.

"This report clearly shows the importance of even small amounts of cash savings to people on low incomes. Our own research has shown that millions across the UK lack a sufficient savings buffer to protect them from financial shocks – a total of 16.8 million working-age adults have less than £100 in savings accounts. We also know that successful saving is all about finding the right approach for you.

"Toynbee Hall's report shows the variety of savings goals and behaviours that exist across the income spectrum. This research highlights the need to open up a variety of options to allow people to save, particularly for those on low incomes, in ways that work for them."

Jake Eliot, Senior Policy Manager
at the Money Advice Service

"Informal savings techniques do not show up on official statistics, and very often go hidden. Many low income households don't even recognise their methods as 'savings' per se, more like money they are just not spending or putting aside for a rainy day.

"When we spoke to people about their methods, we found that making informal savings made people think about how far they could make their money go, even if they were struggling. It also allowed them to prepare for unforeseen events and expenses."

Carl Packman, Toynbee Hall's
Research and Good Practice
Manager and the author
of the report

22 March 2017

⇨ The above information is reprinted with kind permission from Toynbee Hall and Carl Packman, the author of the report. Please visit www.toynbeehall.org.uk for further information.

Looking after the pennies

An extract from a Royal London study into the impact of regular monitoring on household spending and saving.

Executive summary

We all want to make the most of our money. Yet 19 million people in the UK don't have an approach to budgeting they feel works and many struggle to manage their day-to-day money[1]. Saving and setting aside money for emergencies can be hard and it's estimated that 21 million people in the UK have less than £500 in savings to cover unexpected bills like mending a boiler or replacing a fridge[2].

At Royal London we wanted to look at whether budgeting tools could help people manage their money better. To do this we asked a selection of our customers to use a mobile phone budgeting app or a simple pen and paper method to create and keep a budget for three months. We asked them about their budgeting habits and how they manage their finances at the start of the study and then again at the end. In addition we ran forums and interviewed some of the participants.

In this report we present our findings and conclusions.

Key findings

⇨ At the start of the study, 93% recognised the importance of tracking household expenditure and 84% told us they felt in control of their finances.

⇨ While people recognise the importance of budgeting, that doesn't always mean they do and 31% said they don't plan their spending closely or at all.

⇨ Although the majority felt in control of their finances, 30% reported struggling to keep up with bills.

---

1. UK Financial Capability Survey, Money Advice Service, 2015. See www.fincap.org.uk/uk-financial-capability-strategy-is-launched.

2. Ibid.

⇨ At the end of the trial, one in two (49%) said that using a budgeting method was helpful in monitoring what they spend.

⇨ More than one in three (37%) said that since using a budgeting method they have a better understanding of their income and expenditure.

⇨ Around one in four (26%) said they are now more likely to discuss their household finances with their partner/ family/household.

⇨ Financially vulnerable people seem to have benefitted most from the exercise.

⇨ After taking part in the trial, a slightly higher proportion of our sample:

- more closely planned their spending

- claimed to have a clear idea of how to create a weekly/ monthly budget

- were more aware of how much they spend and on what

- could pay an unexpected bill of £300 out of their own money without dipping into savings or cutting back on essentials.

Because of the relatively small sample sizes, we cannot conclusively say that our study proves that budgeting was the cause of these changes. But from talking to the individual participants in the research we know that some of them certainly found the process of monitoring their spending helpful.

Many people found the process time-consuming but those that stuck with it saw real benefits – in particular we found they were thinking more carefully before spending money and cutting back on non-essential spending.

Examples include:

⇨ using cheaper supermarkets

⇨ cycling rather than using public transport

⇨ cancelling old subscriptions

⇨ giving up smoking

⇨ buying a coffee machine rather than takeouts

⇨ cutting down on takeaway meals

⇨ watching how much electricity they used.

Several participants also said they were now saving more and even those on low incomes and the tightest of budgets often reported being able to make savings.

Our research results will contribute to the growing body of evidence that the Money Advice Service is collating about what does and doesn't work to improve financial capability in the UK.

2015

⇨ The above information is reprinted with kind permission from The Royal London. Please visit www. royallondon.com for further information

How to have the awkward conversation – no, not about sex

By Iona Bain

It's that awkward conversation many parents dread – no, not about sex, but money. It is one of the most valuable discussions you can have, but a worrying number of parents shy away from talking about financial issues, according to research for Times *Money*. About half of these parents believe that they don't have the knowledge or the confidence to pass on financial wisdom, while a quarter say they don't have time.

The survey, by Experian and the Personal Finance Education Group, found that most families believe schools should be doing more to enlighten the next generation. Personal finance became a compulsory part of the curriculum in 2014, but only for those children in maintained secondary schools.

Academies and free schools, heavily championed by the Government in recent years, do not have to follow the national curriculum; this could explain why only 26 per cent of pupils received lessons on money last year.

Here are ten tips for teaching your children about money.

Primary-school age

⇨ Explain what money is

Children form financial attitudes by the age of eight, according to research from Cambridge University. Start the ball rolling by getting your kids to count the coins and notes in your purse, says Michael Mercieca, the chief executive of the charity Young Enterprise. "Talk about the different sizes, colours and numbers on them, and how many different coins and notes there are."

Explain that money is a currency that we all need to pay for things. Lynn James, the founder of the Mrs Mummypenny blog and mum of three boys, says: "It's important to understand the value of money. I always explain how much things cost, from a pair of football

boots to the mortgage. It puts thing into perspective."

⇨ Discuss the world of work

Understanding the connection between working and money is vital. Mr Mercieca says: "Talk to them about where money comes from. We're an increasingly cashless society, and thanks to cashback it's easy for children to assume that the supermarket is the source of all of your funds. Showing your child your payslip and explaining what you had to do to find employment is helpful."

Ms James says: "I am open about how much money we earn as a family and explain how different jobs can earn different amounts of money."

⇨ Earning is learning

Children aged between eight and 12 should earn their own money by doing simple tasks such as dusting and washing the dishes. Alex Zivoder, the chief executive at the children's debit-card company goHenry, recommends

setting a base rate and then operating a "pay by chore" model.

"If they accept a task, set them a deadline. If the work isn't done, make sure you explain that they only get the money if the work is done and give them another chance to do it." As a guideline, the average weekly allowance for an eight-year-old is £4.44, rising to £5.22 for nine-year-olds and £5.65 for 11-year-olds

⇨ Start saving

Set up a savings account for your child and make sure they are involved from the start. Coax them into saving at least ten per cent of their weekly allowance. To boost the habit, you could offer them 50p for every £1 saved. Ask them to write down their spending goals; do they know how much they need and how long they would need to save for? And don't talk down saving, even if interest rates are meagre. The personal-finance charity MyBnk reckons that if your child saves £3.75 a week, from the age of seven, at four per cent interest they would have £1,600 in the bank by age 15.

Angela Cork, who runs Ringwood Fabrics in Hampshire, has her sons Sam, 15, and Merlin, 11, helping out in the shop, and cashing up at the end of the day and pays their pocket money into the online bank account GoHenry.

"If Sam goes to the cinema with friends, I like the fact that my phone pings and I can see when and where he's using his card," she says. "One of the best things is you can set tasks and goals, which if they achieve they can see has earned them money.

"If they are nice to their brother, if they unload the dishwasher or keep their room tidy, I can reward them. One day Sam was particularly helpful round the house, painting and clearing out. I sent him a fiver which came up on his phone with a message saying thanks for your help today.

"They also think a little more about whether they want to get that great big popcorn thing if the cost is there in black and white on their phone."

⇨ Don't do handouts

Once you have settled on an allowance, don't waver. Mr Zivoder says: "If you give kids top-ups when they run out, they may feel they can spend their pocket money, knowing that they'll get more. Making choices and learning to prioritise is important. Help younger children to consider which option is best."

Sharan Jaswal, the education director at MyBnk, says: "Parents can ask their kids: 'Would you rather have four treats now and none for the rest of the month, or one four times a week?' Stick to your guns and repeat the lesson," he says, adding that you should leave the door open for children to negotiate a higher allowance if they can make a worthy case for it.

"This is a good way of preparing them for workplace salary negotiations."

Secondary-school children

⇨ Get budgeting

Once your child reaches secondary school, they should be allowed to spend their monthly allowance however they want, but make sure they can pay for necessary expenses, such as lunches, etc. They should be in the habit of tracking their monthly income and outgoings (including savings). They should also write down how much they want to spend on discretionary items or projects they want to save for.

⇨ Wean them off the Bank of Mum and Dad

Mr Zivoder suggests switching from paid chores to a proper part-time job outside the home as children get older. Paying the allowance only once a month will provide an extra nudge. Encourage your kids to use their skills and pursue their interests.

⇨ Give them financial responsibility

Involve your kids in the weekly shop and get them to choose the best-value items you need. You could give them any of the money left over as a reward if they come in under budget.

Mr Mercieca also advises looking at utility bills together, to explore the cost of running a home. Teenagers could even be tasked with switching your utilities online.

Vivi Friedgut, the author of *Money Smarter – A Family Guide*, says: "Encourage them to look at all elements of switching, and foster critical thinking by getting them to read the small print." Include them in conversations about buying big items, such as a TV. Mr Zivoder says: "Get them to do the research and discuss the things to consider when making a purchase."

⇨ Get down to specifics

Ms James advises explaining the difference between renting and mortgages. Youngsters can start to save into a Help to Buy Isa from the age of 16. Parents shouldn't be afraid to discuss the basics of investing either. "The concept of a share is the simplest to explain," says Mrs James. You might even want to talk to your school about entering a school share competition, such as shares4schools.co.uk.

⇨ Tackle debt

Young people heading off to university can be bamboozled by easy credit. Ms James says: "No teenager should think of a credit card as 'free money'. Talk to them about the costs in terms of interest and how it must be paid back." Explain why payday loans and gambling are bad news. Ms Friedgut says: "The sooner young people learn of the dangers, the better."

Best money websites for juniors

Your kids are growing up in an increasingly cashless world, so don't fall behind the times.

It might make sense to use an online piggy bank such as Qwiddle (qwiddle.co.uk). You can set paid chores through the site's dashboard, deposit money safely into your child's account using PayPal and let them set their own saving goals. Only you are allowed to authorise their spending in vetted online stores.

"Kids of all ages can top up what they're learning at school through the Top Marks website. It provides interactive money games and links to helpful external resources, notably the Counting on Money programme, sponsored by the Nationwide building society"

For older kids, Osper (osper.com) is a handy debit card and budgeting app rolled into one. The advantage for parents? They can download the app and send money to their children's debit cards on the go.

If you want your children to learn more about the stock market, the Fantasy Stock Exchange (fantasystockexchange.biz) is a fun and informative website that turns investing into a competition; winners receive a £250 voucher to spend at Hamleys.

16 August 2016

⇨ The above information is an extract reprinted with kind permission from The Young Money Blog. Please visit www.youngmoneyblog.co.uk for further information

© 2017 The Young Money Blog

Four out of ten adults are not in control of their finances – new strategy launched to improve UK's financial capability

An extract from a Press Release from the Money Advice Service.

⇨ Around four out of ten adults are not in control of their finances

⇨ One in five cannot read a bank statement

⇨ Four in ten adults have less than £500 in savings

⇨ One in three cannot calculate the impact of a 2% annual interest rate on £100 in savings

Leading figures from across the financial services industry, government, third sector organisations and charities have come together to launch a major initiative to address the stubbornly low levels of financial capability in the UK.

The Money Advice Service, in conjunction with the UK Financial Capability Board, has today published a ten year Financial Capability Strategy which aims to improve people's ability to manage money well day to day, prepare for and manage life events, and deal with financial difficulties. Its focus will be on developing people's financial skills and knowledge as well as their attitudes and motivation.

Based on extensive research among 5,000 people and consultation with key organisations and institutions, the Financial Capability Strategy spells out in stark terms the problems the nation faces and the approach we must take to resolve them.

Key research findings include:

⇨ Only half of families have any life cover

⇨ 21 million don't have a modest £500 in savings to cover unexpected bills like replacing the fridge or mending the car

⇨ 19 million don't have an approach to budgeting that they feel works

⇨ Around eight million have problems with debt : of those, just one in six is seeking help

In practice this means a "spend today rather than save for tomorrow" culture, limited financial resilience to deal with unexpected life events, and financial difficulties that are closely associated with mental health problems.

To address this, the strategy focuses on every key life stage and challenge: children and young people, young adults, working age people, savings, retirement planning, older people, and people in financial difficulties. Specific actions for the devolved nations will be delivered in Scotland, Wales and Northern Ireland.

The strategy is built around two key concepts:

i. collective impact and cross-sector co-ordination rather than isolated interventions

ii. testing and learning to determine what works in order to deliver evidence-based interventions: resources will be steered towards activities on the basis of what is proven to work.

Overall progress will be monitored by a Financial Capability Survey and ongoing evaluation of specific interventions.

Commenting on the launch of the Strategy, Andy Briscoe, Chairman of the Financial Capability Board said:

"Four out of ten adults are not in control of their finances, so for a great many people money is a constant source of worry and stress. This is a problem first and foremost for the individuals concerned and for their families, but it also has wider implications for society and the economy. The stubbornly low levels of financial capability in the UK can no longer be tolerated. Today we are calling for a fully collaborative approach to ensure we achieve the goals set out in the Strategy over the next decade."

28 October 2015

⇨ The above information is reprinted with kind permission from Money Advice Service. Please visit www. moneyadviceservice.org.uk for further information

© *2017 Money Advice Service*

UK household debt to hit a record £15,000 as wages stagnate

Families are increasingly turning to credit cards and payday loans to pay bills, says TUC.

By Roger Baird

Household debt in the UK is set to jump to £15,000 by 2020, with families increasingly turning to credit cards and payday loans to make ends meet, according to the TUC.

The union's research is based on the most recent data from the Office for National Statistics and government finances watchdog the Office for Budget Responsibility.

It added that unsecured debt per household is set to reach a record high of £13,900 this year, rising from £13,200 last year. This comes at a time when rising inflation is outpacing wage growth.

These levels are only marginally below the peak of £13,300 in 2007, set at the beginning of the financial crisis.

The TUC said: "Wages in the UK are still worth around £20 per week less than before the financial crisis a decade ago. The next government will inherit an economy that is heavily reliant on household spending to maintain growth, but in which debt per household is higher than before the financial crisis."

The amount of county court debt judgements leapt by 35% to almost 300,000 in England and Wales over the first three months of 2017, the highest quarterly figure for more than ten years, according to data from the Registry Trust released last week.

Consumer credit rose by £1.4 billion in February, reflecting an annual growth rate of 10.5%, according to recent data from the Bank of England.

Warnings on debt

In recent months the Bank of England, MPs and charities have warned that consumer debt levels were dangerously high, citing increases in lending from banks, car leasing companies, credit card firms and shops offering interest free-credit.

TUC general secretary Frances O'Grady said: "The surge in household debt is putting the economy in the danger zone.

"We've got this problem because wages haven't recovered. Credit cards and payday loans are helping to prop up household spending for now, but millions of families are running on empty.

"The next government must act urgently to deliver the higher wages Britain needs for sustainable growth. They must boost the minimum wage, and end pay restrictions for public servants like nurses, firefighters and midwives."

24 May 2017

⇨ The above information is reprinted with kind permission from the *International Business Times*. Please visit www.ibtimes.co.uk for further information.

Five million working people struggle with money worries

Nearly five million working Brits are worried about their financial situation, according to research by consumer group Which?

By Joanna Faith

In total, 28% of all UK house-holds said they experience some form of financial stress be it relying more on overdrafts and loans or struggling to pay bills.

But among working households, the figure jumped to 61%.

"In total, 28% of all UK house-holds said they experience some form of financial stress be it relying more on overdrafts and loans or struggling to pay bills"

The most common forms of financial distress for working and struggling households were a reliance on more traditional types of borrowing. Some 20% of people had a loan or credit card, had borrowed money from friends and family, or had used authorised overdrafts as well as cutting back. One in five people had defaulted on a loan, bill, mortgage payment or rent.

Nearly two fifths of these households thought their financial situation would get worse in the next year. The top worries for these people were levels of household debt, fuel prices, housing costs, the prices of food and levels of savings.

Vicki Sheriff, Which? director of campaigns and communications, said: "It's alarming to see how millions of working households in the UK are struggling financially. Many are worried about paying their rent, mortgages, everyday household bills and loans. What's worse, is that one in five of these households are relying on credit cards, overdrafts and the goodwill of their friends and family to help them get by.

"At a time when people are feeling the pinch, we are urging the Government to use its upcoming Budget to consider how it can deliver measures that will help those families that are working and struggling with money worries."

1 March 2017

⇨ The above information is reprinted with kind permission from Your Money. Please visit www.yourmoney.com for further information.

© 2017 Your Money

Britain in the Red

Why we need action to help over-indebted households.

An extract from the Trades Union Congress report

Executive summary

It is now over eight years since the onset of the global financial crisis and the Great Recession. Private indebtedness is widely understood as a major underlying cause of the crisis, as high-risk loans and sub-prime mortgages fatally undermined the stability of major financial institutions. While there has been a good deal of emphasis since 2008 on the household elements of private debt, this has tended to be dominated by mortgage debt. The 'Britain in the Red' project was set up to look in more detail at what has happened to households' use of consumer credit.

Households borrow either to spread their spending over a longer period, or when their everyday costs cannot be covered by their income. With households experiencing an unprecedented decline in real earnings, the obvious concern is that more households are finding themselves unable to cover their living costs without taking on debt. In the wake of the very large build-up of debts on consumer credit over the decade from 1997 to 2007, they are also find existing repayment costs significantly harder to manage

While there has been some improvement in overall levels of indebtedness since debt peaked ahead of the crisis, unsecured borrowing began to rise from 2014 and is forecast by the OBR to return to its peak in five years' time.

Total unsecured debt for UK households (which includes credit cards, payday loans etc and student loans. but not mortgages) rose by £48bn between 2012 and 2015 to reach £353bn. Unsecured debt previously peaked at £364bn in 2008 and fell in the recession. The increase since 2012 increase is in part due to the major extension of student loans.

Consumer credit (i.e. household borrowing excluding both student loans and mortgages) peaked in 2008 at £230bn; it fell back to £184bn in 2012, but had risen again to £212 by the end of 2015. Bank of England figures now show consumer credit growing at an annual rate of ten per cent, the highest for over ten years.

This report shows that many conventional measures may understate the scale of these debts and the burdens associated with repayment, due to complexities in the National Accounts measures of household debt, the increased role of student loans and the treatment of loan rescheduling and write-offs. In addition, in terms of households' ability to meet the cost of interest payments, conventional measures do not take into account recent increases in the costs of living. The report therefore suggests alternative measures of indebtedness. In particular a new measure of debt servicing is derived, showing interest payments as a share of a household sector 'surplus' – that is, the amount that households have left to meet the cost of debt payments once living costs have been taken into account. This suggests the burden of indebtedness has risen in recent years in contrast to falls on the conventional measure. On this basis, interest payments on unsecured borrowing are at an all-time high, and are high relative to other countries.

This high burden comes as the cumulative effect of previous indebtedness is exacerbated by the fragility of household finances since the crisis. While spending has risen more slowly than before the crisis, it has come alongside greatly reduced income growth in the wake of the earnings crisis.

While these figures are indicative of pressures on the economy as a whole, the most significant impact is distributional. The discussion is based on two measures.

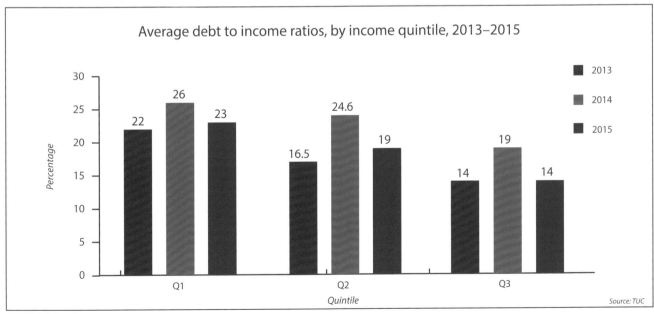

Financial vulnerability

Financially vulnerable households have debts that are worth 60 per cent of their income. Since the preliminary report was published in September 2015 there has been an improvement in measures of vulnerability, as wage growth picked up in 2015. However measures remain elevated and the acceleration in wage growth already appears short-lived.

Moreover, the lowest income decile is considerably more vulnerable. In 2015 the unsecured debt to income ratio of lowest income households was 22 per cent, seven times as high as the ratio of those in the highest income group.

Over indebtedness

Households in problem debt have to spend more than 25 per cent of their monthly income paying the interest on their debts (credit cards, loans, overdrafts, arrears).

Correspondingly there has also been some improvement in debt servicing measures and hence over-indebtedness into 2015, though measures are still severely elevated relative to 2012.

Overall, 11 per cent of households holding any form of unsecured debt are estimated as over-indebted in 2015, more than double compared to the five per cent in 2012. Of the over-indebted households, half are extremely over-indebted and so paying out more than 40 per cent of their income to their unsecured creditors.

In total, 3.2 million households or 7.6 million people are over-indebted, an increase of 700,000 or 28 per cent since 2012. On this basis nearly one in eight of all UK households are currently over-indebted. Likewise, 1.6 million households are in 'extreme debt'.

For households earnings £30,000 or less, 16 per cent were over indebted in 2015 the same as in 2014 and up from nine per cent in 2012.

However, the share of extremely over-indebted low income households rose to nine per cent in 2015, up from eight per cent in 2014 and three times as many as in 2012. Overall, 1.2 million low income households are estimated to be in extreme problem debt.

Even more worrying is that extreme

over-indebtedness is growing particularly quickly in low income households that are in employment (excluding self-employment).

In 2015, nine per cent of low income households in employment were extremely over-indebted, up from five per cent in 2014.

The final section includes conclusions and recommendations.

Following the discussion of the measurement of household indebtedness, proposals are made for future monitoring of the household debt burden and also actions to facilitate reducing this burden.

⇨ Improve the monitoring of the household debt burden.

⇨ Establish a target to reduce the household debt burden.

⇨ Implement effective measures to achieve the target.

Most obviously actions are needed to strengthen household incomes through higher wages. These should follow from actions to strengthen

the economy, including increased infrastructure spending and the development and implementation of an industry plan. Specifically on debt, actions should build on existing re-packaging and refinancing initiatives to reduce both the stock of household debt and the interest paid on consumer credit liabilities. We argue that if the government took a more active role more progress could be made in both reducing the pressures on households and also in strengthening banks' revenues. The government should also review the current debt advice and insolvency system, with the aim of a system that is cheap to access and provides sufficient protections to enable a fresh start.

2016

⇨ The above information is reprinted with kind permission from the Trades Union Congress. Please visit www.yourmoney.com for further information

A look at the lives of half a million people in debt in the UK

Demand for debt advice

The highest demand, both in absolute terms and relative to population, came from London. 102,133 people from the capital sought debt assistance in 2016, the equivalent of 150 people per 10,000.

The next highest level of demand compared to population came from the North East, where we advised 134 clients per 10,000.

In 2016 there were 3.3 million visits to the charity's website, an increase of more than 100% over five years.

What debts do people have?

The average debt of our clients earning less than £30,000 increased by £569, to £12,897, in 2016. Over the same period, the average debt of clients earning more than £30,000 decreased by £2,160 to £29,340. Because those earning less make up a far higher proportion of our client base, this means that for the first time in eight years the overall average unsecured debt of our clients increased, from £13,900 to £14,251.

On average clients have 5.7 unsecured debts, including almost three credit cards. Overall, more than two-thirds of clients owe money on credit cards and over half have overdraft debts.

The amount of debt owed on catalogues, personal loans, store cards, home credit and payday loans increased between 2015 and 2016.

In addition to unsecured credit commitments, four in ten people are behind on their household bills. This is an increase of 5% over the last five years. On top of their unsecured debts, this amounts to an additional average debt burden of £2,061 for these clients.

Debt owed by clients to their family and friends continues to grow rapidly. Last year, 28.3% of clients owed money to a relative or friend. In total they owed almost £434 million. This is £135 million more than they owed in 2015.

Who's seeking advice?

The proportion of clients aged under 40 continued to grow in 2016. They now account for 60% of all clients advised. Five years ago it was 52%. One in five clients is a single parent. This is double the proportion of single parents in the UK population.

The proportion of clients who rent their home has grown from 61% to 78% in just five years. The fastest growth in demand has come from those living in private rented accommodation who now account for almost four in ten clients.

Family wage income continues to stagnate. Average client household take home pay not including benefits income in 2016 was £46 less per month than it was five years ago.

Wage stagnation means the number of clients unable to cover essential outgoings has continued to rise. Even after a budgeting session, 29% of clients in 2016 did not have enough to cover all essential bills at the end of the month.

2016

⇨ The above information is reprinted with kind permission from StepChange Debt Charity. Please visit www.stepchange.org for further information

Young people bearing the brunt of Britain's debt

⇨ Polling reveals 55% of 18- to 24-year-olds and 48% of 25-34 yos say debt increasing, compared to only 13% of over-65s

⇨ "Unexpected expenses" and "affording the basics" are most common money worries

⇨ Findings come ahead of a major study into the impact of debt on Britain's homes

Over three times as many young people than pensioners are bearing the brunt of increasing debt, according to new findings revealed by the think tank Demos.

55% of 18–24-year-olds, and 48% of 25–34 year olds, said that their debt had increased over the past five years, compared to only 13% of over-65s. In comparison, only 12% of 18–24 year olds, and 28% of 25–34 year olds, saw their debt decrease during the same The findings come from a Demos poll of 1,775 adults released ahead of a comprehensive report on the 'real-life' impact of debt due to be published next month.

Respondents were asked to calculate the full extent of their debt, including credit cards, rent and bill arrears, and any combination of bank, student or payday loans

The majority of young people said they had over £2,000 of debt. However, a fifth (19%) of both 18–24 year olds and almost a quarter (22%) of 25–34 year olds revealed they currently owe in excess of £10,000.

The figures present a bleak scenario for young adults already facing pressure from a cost of living squeeze, rising rents and the Government's welfare and housing benefit reforms.

Demos researchers found that although there may be positive reasons for getting into debt – such as funding their studies – the reasons are much more likely to be negative, with many struggling to make ends meet at the end of each month.

Amongst 25–34-year-olds: 35% got into debt due to 'unexpected expenses', 28% couldn't 'afford the basics', while 27% cited a 'one-off purchase'.

Of the 18–24-year-olds surveyed, less than a third (30%) put their rising debt down to positive reasons such as "investing in their future", despite being the most likely group to have taken a student loan. 28% cited "unexpected expenses", 27% to "afford the basics" and 18% to cover their rent.

Jo Salter, a researcher at Demos who led the project, said:

"When we talk about rising debt levels, it is young people in their 20s and 30s who are bearing the brunt. This is a time in their lives when previous generations would be thinking about starting a family or trying to get on the property ladder. Instead of saving for the future, they are being dragged into debt just to meet the costs of living.

"It's a common mistake to assume that all debt is equally bad for all people. Demos is trying to uncover some of the differences between peoples' experience of debt, based on the various ways it affects them – from legal consequences to emotional distress to the risk of finances flying out of control in the longer term.

"In this way, providers of advice and support to people in debt can move away from treating everyone the same and towards a more tailored response, designed to tackle specific impacts of debt."

19 April 2016

⇨ The above information is reprinted with kind permission from Demos. Please visit www.demos.co.uk for further information.

Financial inclusion

Introduction

Financial inclusion means belonging to a modern mainstream financial system that is fit-for-purpose for everyone, regardless of their income. It is essential for anyone wanting to participate fairly and fully in everyday life. Without access to appropriate mainstream financial services, people pay more for goods and services and have less choice. The impacts of exclusion are not just financial but also affect education, employment, health, housing, and overall well-being.

Who is financially excluded?

While financial exclusion affects a wide range of people at different times in their lives, it mainly impacts people with low or unstable incomes, or who have experienced a significant life shock. Lone parents, single pensioners, migrants, long-term sick or disabled people, the long-term unemployed, and households headed by students or part-time workers are some of the groups most commonly excluded from financial services.

The facts

Banking

⇨ Internationally, the UK is ranked ninth in the world in terms of banking inclusion by the World Bank.[1]

⇨ 1.5 million adults remain unbanked in Britain today.[2]

⇨ Only about half of the unbanked would like a bank account.[3]

⇨ Some 50% of the newly banked have incurred penalty fees, with those affected averaging 5.6 charges per year.[4] 26% of the newly banked are 'net losers', incurring more penalty charges than they have gained in savings.[5]

⇨ Around half of people with a basic bank account choose to manage their money in cash.[6]

⇨ 60–67% of the unbanked[7] and 40–60% of the newly banked[8] have previously had an account. Around 15% of newly opened accounts are closed or abandoned.[9]

⇨ Customer satisfaction levels are below 60% for the four largest providers.[10]

⇨ Between 1989 and 2012, more than 40% of all bank and building society branches have closed – a net loss of 7,500 branches. Low income areas have disproportionately borne the brunt of these closures.[11]

1. World Bank, 2012. Financial Inclusion Data: Global Findex Database. [Online] Available at: http://datatopics.worldbank.org/financialinclusion/ [Accessed 23 August 2014].

2. Rowlingson, K. & McKay, S., 2014. Financial Inclusion: Annual monitoring report 2014, Birmingham: University of Birmingham.

3. Financial Inclusion Taskforce, 2010. Banking Services and Poorer Households, London: Financial Inclusion Taskforce.

4. Ellison, A., Whyley, C. & Forster, R., 2010. Realising Banking Inclusion: The achievements and challenges, London: HM Treasury.

5. Ibid,

6. Social Finance, 2011. A New Approach to Banking: Extending the use of Jam Jar Accounts in the UK, London: Social Finance.

7. Financial Inclusion Taskforce, 2010. Banking Services and Poorer Households, London: Financial Inclusion Taskforce; Ellison, A., Whyley, C. & Forster, R., 2010. Realising Banking Inclusion: The achievements and challenges, London: HM Treasury.

8. Ibid; Kempson, E. & Collard, S., 2012. Developing a Vision for Financial Inclusion, Dorking: Friends Provident Foundation.

9. Ellison, A., Whyley, C. & Forster, R., 2010. Realising Banking Inclusion: The achievements and challenges, London: HM Treasury; Financial Inclusion Taskforce, 2010. Banking Services and Poorer Households, London: Financial Inclusion Taskforce.

10. Competition and Markets Authority, 2014. Personal Current Accounts: Market study updates, London: Competition and Markets Authority.

11 French, S., Leshon, A. & Meek, S., 2013. The Changing Geography of British Bank and Building Society Branch Networks 2003–12, Nottingham: University of Nottingham.

Whether any accounts	2008–09	2009–10	2010–2011	2011–12	2012–13	2013–14
Yes	44,828,296	45,147,566	45,890,210	46,295,434	46,986,457	46,410,058
No	995,897	1,008,048	871,287	868,038	926,049	1,314,714
Don't know	1,660,962*	271,796	242,451	329,949	416,629	460,057
Refused		1,215,075	1,019,666	1,007,548	1,161,829	1,341,454

Did you have now, or have you had at any time in the last 12 months any accounts? This could be in your own name only, or held jointly with someone else. Include internet/phone accounts. *Family Resources Survey*

* In 2008/09 the missing codes (refused and don't know) were not separate.

Credit

⇨ An estimated two million people took out a high-cost loan in 2012 as they were unable to access any other form of credit.[12]

⇨ The level of unsecured consumer credit has tripled in the past 20 years, from £51.8 billion in 1993 to £160.4 billion in 2014.[13]

⇨ It is estimated that 49–64% of households in the UK hold some form of unsecured credit.[14]

⇨ It is estimated that between three million[15] to seven million[16] households use high-cost credit.

⇨ The payday lending market has grown from £330 million in 2006 to £3.7 billion in 2012.[17]

⇨ The pawnbroking market has grown from £296 million in 2007 to £821 million in 2012.[18]

⇨ The number of illegal money-lenders is estimated to have risen from 165,000 in 2006 to 310,000 in 2010.[19]

Savings

There are 13 million people in the UK who do not have enough savings to support them for one month if they experienced a 25% cut in income.[20]

Only 41% of British households are saving.[21]

The UK saves less than almost any other country in the EU.[22]

Insurance

Half of households in the bottom half of the income distribution lack home contents insurance, compared with one in five households on average incomes.[23]

Households with no home contents insurance were more than three times as likely to be burgled than those with insurance.[24]

Context

61% of the UK population owns a smartphone.[25]

77% of adults have access to broadband, either fixed or on their mobile.[26]

On average, real wages fell by 9% between 2008 and 2013.[27]

Between 2007 and 2013, electricity, gas, and fuel costs rose by 61%. Over the same period, food prices increased by 31%, and transport costs by 25%.[28]

It is estimated that 2.5 million people will need budgeting support to transition onto Universal Credit's monthly, direct payment.[29]

27 March 2017

⇨ The above information is reprinted with kind permission from the Financial Inclusion Commission. Please visit www.financialinclusioncommission. org. uk for further information.

12. Centre for Social Justice, 2014. Restoring the Balance: Tackling problem debt, London: Centre for Social Justice.

13. Bank of England, 2014. LPQBI2O: Quarterly amounts of outstanding of ttal (excluding the Student Loans Company) sterling net unsecured lending to individuals (in sterling millions) seasonally adjusted, London: Bank of England.

14. Wealth and Assets Survey in Rowlingson, K. & McKay, S., 2014. Financial Inclusion: Annual monitoring report 2014, Birmingham: University of Birmingham.; YouGov poll in BIS, 2010. Over-indebtedness in Britain: second follow-up report, London: Department for Business, Innovation and Skills; NMG survey in Bank of England, 2013. The Financial Position of British Households: Evidence from the 2013 NMG Consulting survey, London: Bank of England.

15. Financial Inclusion Taskforce, 2010. Mainstreaming Financial Inclusion: Planning for the future and coping with financial pressure – access to affordable credit, London: Financial Inclusion Taskforce.

16. Purtill, C., Cray, J. & Mitchell, C., 2011. DWP Credit Union Expansion Project: Feasibility Study Report, London: Department for Work and Pensions.

17. Beddows, S. & McAteer, M., 2014. Payday Lending: Fixing a broken market, London: Association of Chartered Certified Accountants.

18. Reed, J., 2012. The Return of Pawnbroking. BBC News, 20 December, http://www.bbc.co.uk/news/20791776.

19. Policis, 2006. Illegal Lending in the UK, London: Department of Trade and Industry; Policis, 2010. Interim Evaluation of the National Illegal Money Lending Projects, London: Department for Business, Innovation and Skills.

20. StepChange, 2014. Life on the Edge, London: StepChange.

21. Family Resources Survey data in Rowlingson, K. & McKay, S., 2014. Financial Inclusion: Annual monitoring report 2014, Birmingham: University of Birmingham.

22. OECD, 2012. Factbook 2011–12, London: Organisation for Economic Co-operation and Development.

23. Rowlingson, K. & McKay, S., 2014. Financial Inclusion: Annual monitoring report 2014, Birmingham: University of Birmingham.

24. Ibid

25. http://media.ofcom.org.uk/facts/

26. http://media.ofcom.org.uk/facts/

27. Gregg, P., Machin, S. & Fernandez-Salgado, M., 2014. Real Wages and Unemployment in the Big Squeeze. The Economic Journal, 124(May), pp. 408–432.

28. Resolution Foundation, 2014. The State of Living Standards, London: Resolution Foundation.

29. http://www.publications.parliament.uk/pa/cm201213/cmselect/cmworpen/576/57606.htm#n138

How ethnic minorities face higher levels of financial exclusion

An article from **The Conversation.**

THE CONVERSATION

By Alper Kara

Access to financial services and credit is generally regarded as a necessity to lead a normal life. Whether it is basic bank and saving accounts, a mortgage to buy a house or loan to start a business, these are some of the essential components of the modern economy – and modern living.

Yet financial exclusion – the inability to access these financial services – is a problem for many people. And there is mounting research to show that certain sections of society are affected more than others. There are two main areas where access to finance is needed: consumer credit and mortgages. In both areas, there is a large amount of evidence to show that ethnic minorities are worse off than white households.

Financial exclusion plays a critical role in increasing poverty and limiting prosperity for all. The link between ability to access finance and prosperity is a simple one. Take, for example, consumer credit. It enables spending that exceeds our monthly budgets and gives us the ability to stretch the cost of big (and often important) purchases over time. Credit allows us to smooth our income and broaden investment opportunities. This can lead to, for instance, better housing or further education and training.

Access to mortgages is also very important. Being a homeowner is an essential component of wealth acquisition and can increase status and standing in society. Restricted access to finance, on the other hand, can exacerbate economic disadvantage that may lead to social exclusion.

Investigating the causes

Ethnicity is one of many factors that influence access to finance. These include a person's level of income, their net worth, education, employment status and age. Yet in advanced economies, the financially excluded include a disproportionate number of ethnic minorities.

Some credit applicants may be excluded because they do not fulfil the minimum economic criteria (such as insufficient income, net worth and so on). But there may also be discrimination on non-economic grounds.

Financial exclusion has been widely researched in the United States, particularly access to mortgages. Studies show that ethnic minorities – in particular African Americans and Hispanics – not only have lower access to mortgage funding, but they pay more for mortgages when they get them and are more likely to be subject to predatory lending practices. Findings for consumer credit is not as clear-cut, but there is a strong indication that minorities often face disadvantages.

Racial prejudice is also an issue in the UK. Research illustrates economic disparities manifesting themselves in terms of minorities living in poorer-quality housing, worse health and being disadvantaged when it comes to job opportunities. These structural disadvantages faced are most likely fed through into poorer access to finance and financial services.

In a recent paper with my colleagues Solomon Y Deku and Philip Molyneux, we studied 59,000 households in the UK and found there was clear discrimination when it comes to consumer credit. Our analysis found that ethnic minorities are less likely to have consumer credit compared to white households with similar income levels and other characteristics (such as employment, education and age). Even if they are able to obtain financing, their intensity of borrowing is lower compared with white households.

In another recent paper, Philip Molyneux and I also looked at access to mortgages, where we find less inequality. For the average household, there is no difference in the chances of obtaining a mortgage between ethnic minorities and other households, especially at higher income levels. However, black households with low incomes are at a disadvantage in comparison to other households with comparable economic and other characteristics. In contrast, Asian households do not seem to face such inequality.

The exact reasons for this discrimination are unclear. But, its existence is very clear and should be investigated further. Back in 2011, the then deputy prime minister Nick Clegg launched a probe into discriminatory lending practices by banks. He claimed that businesses owned by black Africans were four times more likely to be denied bank loans than "white firms". Research only partly confirms Clegg's claims. Ethnic minority-owned UK businesses are found to be more likely to report problems in obtaining loans. But loan denials are also linked to differences in creditworthiness, rather than ethnic discrimination.

Limited access to financing by ethnic minority businesses may in some cases be due to discouragement rather than overt discrimination by banks – ethnic minority businessmen may stop themselves from applying for loans because they fear prejudicial treatment. The fact that the problem is ongoing, however, warrants further investigation and the non-economic barriers to ethnic minorities obtaining credit must be removed.

6 March 2017

⇨ The above information is reprinted with kind permission from *The Conversation*. Please visit www.theconversation.co.uk for further information.

The party's over for young people, debt laden and risk averse

By Zoe Williams

It's bad news for the drinks industry, but it's mainly bad news for people who think each generation is more feckless than the last: the number of drinkers among 16- to 24-year-olds has dropped sharply. All kinds of drinkers are dying out: the steady drinkers, the binge drinkers, the drinkers-in-training, the social drinkers the bus stop drinkers – the lot.

In a study by the Office for National Statistics, less than half of young people reported drinking anything in the previous week, compared with two-thirds of 45- to 64-year-olds – many of whom are in all likelihood under medical advice to please cut it out, or at least do the nation the favour of lying about it in surveys.

Various theories are floated: changes in religion and ethnicity, changes wrought by social media, student loans – which we'll return to. But a report compiled by the Demos thinktank last year found health to be the most common reason given for this abstemiousness.

Health has got to them all, like a cult: they are also less likely to smoke, and the evidence of our own five senses gives us young people in hordes jogging, climbing, journeying eternally from one institution of wellness to another, serious-faced in Lycra, taking responsibility, counting footsteps, living the dream. They must look at previous generations, the lad and ladette (read "beer") culture of the 90s, and wonder who on earth we thought we were.

There's plenty to apologise for about the fin de siècle, and it can't all be blamed on Tony Blair, whatever his biographers tell you. It was the end of ideology, the decade sincerity died. Feminists went underground, too postmodern (also, in fairness, too drunk) to explain that just because Margaret Thatcher was a woman it didn't mean she was a passionate advocate of gender equality; and "girl power" was a poor substitute for female emancipation.

The legions of the "post-ironic" never had to account for their vapid agenda or explain the meaning of the term, since it would have been deeply passe to expect one. I say "their"; I mean "our": there must have been postmodernism refuseniks, but I wasn't one of them. It was a creed of puckish underachievement, personal debt, slacking and loafing, with authenticity rejected in favour of acerbic cynicism. The epic hangovers of its breakfast show DJs made national news.

It was, paradoxically, both trivial and destructive. But we never went jogging. Measuring your own recovery time, having a personal best: these were the niche concerns of the elite athlete, as irrelevant to the general youth population as blood doping. It would have been considered vain to the point of alienation to prioritise your workout over your social life. That may be a modern question for new media to answer: that as everyone is ever more on display standards of physical perfection are driven inexorably, needlessly, upwards.

But, crucially, we were without this mantra of personal responsibility, in which everyone must constantly strive towards self-sufficiency and self-improvement. It wasn't because we hadn't heard of it or didn't understand it, or because Nike didn't exist or British Military Fitness hadn't been invented.

We all remembered Thatcher's fascination with the "vigorous values" (energy, adventurousness, independence) over the "softer virtues" (humility, gentleness, sympathy). We had lived through the 80s, the decade in which self-sufficiency reached such an ugly apex of valorisation that it had its own, completely erroneous, catchphrase: greed is good.

We understood the fault line between those two visions of society: the one in which you parade your morals with rigorous self-discipline and concrete, measurable ambitions versus the one in which both morals and ambitions were for losers – and chose the second. It wasn't perfect, but it was better than the first.

Underpinning this new seriousness, this new competitiveness, is a very grave set of circumstances: student debt will change for ever the way 16- to 24-year-olds live, and will continue to do so until we find another way to finance education.

I don't think debt has a particular bearing on alcohol budget but it drives behaviour in more profound ways: people can still afford a pint, but they can't afford to fall behind. To embrace risk, to have a sense of freedom and possibility, a faith in failure as a learning curve, an interest in activities – drinking, say, or chatting – whose productivity can't be measured, perhaps because they aren't productive at all, is plain illogical when you're living in the economic conditions of this generation.

Under the guise of saving them from the burden of the national debt, we have as a society saddled each one, individually, with impossible personal finances, from life-altering debts to career-changing rents and scant or, at the start, nonexistent wages.

The solution is possibly not, at this stage, to get them all drinking more. But we should recognise in trends like these the fact that conditions for this generation are worse. The reasons are systemic, have nothing to do with personal responsibility and cannot be answered by fitness, however extreme.

The drinks industry seeks to solve the conundrum of the monastic twentysomething by "premiumisation" (getting them to spend more on the few drinks they will buy). We have to understand it as a challenge broader than the market, recognise that all of our welfare is all of our business and, out of penance for the decade that made fellowship a joke, show some solidarity now.

19 April 2016

⇨ The above information is reprinted with kind permission from *The Guardian*. Please visit www.theguardian.com for further information.

Students struggling under debt-stress while at university

⇨ Research by financial technology company Intelligent Environments finds three quarters of university students polled feel stressed about the amount of debt they are accumulating whilst studying

⇨ One in seven students surveyed have been chased by debt collectors and over a quarter have missed rent payments

⇨ Students admit debt-stress affects relationships, exam results and ability to afford basics such as weekly food shops

⇨ Banks can play a role to address the situation by providing students with the necessary digital tools to help them keep on top of their outgoings, with half (48 per cent) saying they would be less likely to get into debt with a digital app

It's no secret that students get into debt whilst at university, but new research has found an overwhelming majority are feeling the stress created by their financial situation.

According to financial technology company Intelligent Environments, three quarters (75 per cent) of students polled that receive a maintenance loan feel stressed about the amount of debt they are accumulating while studying, the effects of which are wide reaching.

Over a third (39 per cent) said their debt has prevented them from being able to afford their weekly food shop, whilst over a quarter (27 per cent) have missed rent payments. A worrying 15 per cent have even been chased by debt collectors, demonstrating the severity of the issue.

Psychologically, the debt-stress students experience has impacted various areas of their lives, including relationships (35 per cent), friendships (34 per cent) and exam results (32 per cent).

The study highlights that almost three in five students polled (58 per cent) run out of money before their next payment is due, with the average week for student loan funds to run dry being week six.

Defying stereotypes of drunken nights and time spent socialising, the top three items students spend their money on were revealed to be rent (78 per cent), food (69 per cent) and utility bills (47 per cent).

To get by, a significant proportion of students with a maintenance loan surveyed now rely on additional sources of income to get through the term, with two thirds (65 per cent) turning to parents or other family in times of need. Others rely on their student overdrafts (58 per cent), dip into their savings (27 per cent), incur further debts on credit cards (6 per cent) and even take out payday loans (9 per cent) to help tide them over.

Given the impact of debt-stress on students, Intelligent Environments is calling on banks to provide their younger customers with tools designed to help them better manage their finances to help them stay out of debt where possible.

The call to action is supported by the research, which states that over a third (34 per cent) of students polled cite their bank as an organisation that could do more to help. Two thirds (66 per cent) say debt would be less stressful if their bank offered access to a digital money management tool or app to help them manage their maintenance loan incomings and outgoings, and almost half (48 per cent) believe they would be less likely to go into debt in the first place if they had access to this type of tool.

David Webber, Managing Director at Intelligent Environments, said: "The fact that students are taking on further debts such as credit cards, overdrafts and even payday loans to repay the money they already owe, is worrying. Debt can have a devastating effect on people, impacting everything from exam results to relationships with partners, family and friends.

"Banks need to be doing more to assist students in managing their finances responsibly to help them get through university without having to resort to more forms of borrowing. As younger generations look for digital solutions to keep on top of their spending and debt repayment levels, banks need to adapt and provide students with the digital tools to improve their relationship with money. This will help them keep on top of outgoings and monthly budgets. Greater visibility around spending habits will make people more aware of their bank balance, making it harder for them to go into debt unnecessarily."

Shelly Asquith, National Union of Students (NUS) vice president (welfare), said: "Students are being mounted with colossal levels of debt that are increasing year on year. NUS is concerned about the impact this has on the likelihood of working class students to apply to university. We also believe that increased poverty and debt is a major factor in the sharp increase of students experiencing mental ill health.

"NUS research also shows that almost 60 per cent of graduates still have existing debts left over from their degree, most commonly bank overdrafts, credit cards and loans from friends and family."

21 February 2017

⇨ The above information is an extract reprinted with kind permission from Intelligent Environments. Please visit www.intelligentenvironments for further information

Mobile banking on the rise, thanks to tech-savvy millennials

By Lauren Lyons Cole

The future of banking looks bright, at least for consumers. Tech-savvy millennials are opting for online and mobile banking options over visiting local branches, which will significantly change the way banks do business.

Traditionally, banks have relied heavily on in-person interactions to push products and make sales, but that approach is often better for the bank's bottom line than for the customer's. Banking representatives usually earn sales commissions, which means a customer who walks into a local branch might walk out with an unneeded loan or mutual fund.

"A lot of people have been taken advantage of by the so-called relationship," said Odysseas Papadimitriou, CEO of the personal finance websites WalletHub and CardHub. "You like the person, or you don't like the person, so you're making decisions in a much less rational way."

An increasing number of technology firms are creating digital solutions to the everyday financial problems Americans face, making it easier to avoid the headaches and fees associated with traditional banking. Removing the human touch might leave some nostalgic for a friendlier age, but it could lead to greater wealth accumulation as consumers make decisions based on data, rather than a handshake.

"It's a significant change. Those of us that have a little gray hair tend to think of services that we buy from banks, whereas millennials don't have that at all," said Dean Nicolacakis, a partner at PWC who co-leads the firm's FinTech

practice. "Their presumption is that there has to be some app out there to take care of whatever their needs are."

Banks should take note. Saving is the No. 1 priority for millennials, after paying their monthly bills, according to recent research from Nielsen. More than a third of the American workforce is made up of 18- to 34-year-olds, 27 per cent of whom earn over $75,000 a year.

"Millennials are starting to buy homes and save for retirement and college funding. It's going to have a huge impact in ten years and in 20 years the banking landscape will be completely transformed," Papadimitriou said.

A shift in the way Americans consume financial services is already underway. Wealthfront, an automated online investment advisory service, manages nearly $3 billion. Mobile payment services like Venmo process billions of dollars each year. Simple Bank, one of the few online and mobile-only banks, saw deposits grow by 179 per cent in the past two years alone.

Still, online and mobile banking security is a concern for many consumers, millennials included. Adoption rates continue to rise, but cautiously. In 2014, 52 per cent of smartphone owners engaged in mobile banking, up from 43 per cent in 2011, according to the Federal Reserve Board.

As brick-and-mortar branches become less important, Nicolacakis said he expects to see "banks moving to a model where they're more about goals and helping people hit their goals and less about transactions and accounts". The successful banks will

have to develop a relentless focus on the customer, he said, to keep up with the nimble startups against which they are competing.

Many FinTech companies have already had success implementing the goals-based approach to banking and saving. The average 28-year-old Simple Bank account holder saves ten per cent, well above the negative 1.8 per cent savings rate for Americans under age 35 reported by Moody's Analytics. Sweep, an intelligent budgeting app that can be used with any bank account, uses a similar approach to help make sure users never miss a bill or overspend.

While some are still wrapping their heads around the possibilities for mobile banking, Papadimitriou envisions a future where banks will have to provide services that go beyond a smartphone or tablet app. "You'll be able to talk to your car, to your phone, to your fridge. Your fridge needs to be able to tell you how much you spent on groceries last month," he said. "A bank will have to interface with all of these platforms."

Whatever the innovation, one thing is certain. The future of banking is in the hands of millennials. And that's a good thing.

8 January 2017

⇨ The above information is reprinted with kind permission from *International Business Times*. Please visit www.ibtimes.com for further information

A third of Brits expect this to be last generation using cash

By Stephen Harmston

One in three (34%) think that the country will be cashless within the next 20 years, but many remain reluctant to move away from physical currency due to security concerns about alternatives, new research from YouGov reveals.

The *Cashing In* report looks at how Britain is adapting to alternative payments and which groups need to be convinced about going cashless. It finds that while one in eight (13%) believe the country will do away with cash in the next decade, one in five (21%) reckon it will take between 11 and 20 years. A further fifth believe it will happen in the longer term while three in ten (29%) don't think the country will ever discard physical currency.

YouGov's study highlights the extent to which the country has already adopted a mixed approach to payment methods as various forms of cards and mobile payments take up more of the strain. While four in five (82%) still use cash when in-store, over two thirds (69%) use chip and pin and half (49%) use contactless on their debit cards. Usage of credit cards in various ways is lower.

Furthermore, YouGov's research highlights that frequency of cash use is quite spotty. Only a quarter (26%) of Britons use cash every day, a fifth use it four to six times a week and a third (52%) use it three times a week or less.

This research makes clear that we are heading towards a cashless future. Money – as with everything else – has moved on with technology. The pace and scope of the move away from cash has quickened in recent years with the advent of contactless and mobile payments. With many Britons believing that cash will be dead within a generation, the challenge for financial institutions, retailers and other organisations is to meet this head-on.

Yet while many Britons now used mixed methods to pay for things, there are still large numbers who are sticking with cash because of resistance to more high-tech payment methods. Approaching two thirds (65%) feel that using mobile or cashless payments increases the chance of suffering fraud or theft.

The report highlights particular concerns over mobile payment or deposit systems and apps.

Three in ten (31%) don't think they are secure and a quarter (24%) are concerned about malware and identity theft. Worryingly for those who offer the services, one in six (16%) don't trust providers behind the systems.

However YouGov's study does show how providers will be able to get many more people to try phone payments.

Fully one in five (20%) of those who don't currently use mobile cashless payments would be open to doing so in future.

Despite widespread use of digital transactions, many people are not on board with the idea of a cashless society, so financial institutions and other organisations need to understand these peoples' fears and reassure the sceptics. While older people are more hesitant about paying electronically, we found that those aged 45 to 54 are more likely to be keen on trying mobile payment systems in future. This should help ensure that the move away from cash is not seen as something only for younger generations.

6 July 2017

⇨ The above information is reprinted with kind permission from YouGov. Please visit www.yougov.co.uk for further information.

Virtual Currencies and Beyond: Initial Considerations

Executive Summary.

New technologies – supported by advances in encryption and network computing – are driving transformational change in the global economy, including in how goods, services and assets are exchanged. An important development in this process has been the emergence of virtual currencies (VCs). VC schemes are private sector systems that, in many cases, facilitate peer-to-peer exchange bypassing traditional central clearinghouses. VCs and their associated technologies (notably distributed ledgers based on blockchains) are rapidly evolving, and the future landscape is difficult to predict.

VCs offer many potential benefits, including greater speed and efficiency in making payments and transfers – particularly across borders – and ultimately promoting financial inclusion. The distributed ledger technology underlying some VC schemes – an innovative decentralized means of keeping track of transactions in a large network – offers potential benefits that go far beyond VCs themselves.

At the same time, VCs pose considerable risks as potential vehicles for money laundering, terrorist financing, tax evasion and fraud. While risks to the conduct of monetary policy seem less likely to arise at this stage given the very small scale of VCs, risks to financial stability may eventually emerge as the new technologies become more widely used.

The development of effective regulatory responses to VCs is still at an early stage. VCs are difficult to regulate as they cut across the responsibilities of different agencies at the national level, and operate on a global scale. Many are opaque and operate outside of the conventional financial system, making it difficult to monitor their operations.

Regulators have begun to address these challenges, with a variety of approaches across countries.

Responses have included clarifying the applicability of existing legislation to VCs, issuing warnings to consumers, imposing licensing requirements on certain VC market participants, prohibiting financial institutions from dealing in VCs, completely banning the use of VCs, and prosecuting violators. These approaches represent an initial policy response to the challenges that VCs pose, but further development is needed. In particular, national authorities will need to calibrate regulation in a manner that appropriately addresses the risks without stifling innovation.

More could be done at the international level to facilitate the process of developing and refining policies at the national level. International bodies are playing an important role in identifying and discussing the risks posed by VCs and possible regulatory responses, and they should continue to do so. As experience is gained, international standards and best practices could be considered to provide guidance on the most appropriate regulatory responses in different fields, thereby promoting harmonization across jurisdictions. Such standards could also set out frameworks for cross-country cooperation and coordination in areas such as information sharing and the investigation and prosecution of cross-border offences.

11 January 2016

⇨ The above information is reprinted with kind permission from International Monetary Fund. Please visit www.imf.org/external/pubs/ft/sdn/2016/sdn1603.pdf for further information

Around the world in 80 payments – global moves to a cashless economy

An article from The Conversation.

By Bernardo Batiz-Lazo

Ever since computers were first introduced into the retail banking system in the late 1950s, there has been the vision of a future world where cash is obsolete. The near death of personal cheques, increase in debit and credit card use, and innovations such as PayPal, Square, Apple Pay and bitcoin, have led us to believe the cashless society is well within our reach.

But data from Retail Banking Research, one of the most authoritative sources in the area, suggests that even though cashless payments are growing rapidly across the world, hard currency remains resilient. This trend was corroborated by a study commissioned by the ATM Industry Association of a panel of 30 countries. It suggested that global demand for cash grew 8.9% between 2009 and 2013 (when the latest figures were available).

So 50 years into the journey and we are still not there yet. However, a number of innovations have taken place around the world. Here's how different continents stack up.

Europe

One in ten card payments were contactless for the first time in 2015 in the UK. By making small payments easier and quicker, contactless marks a major threat to cash. London is also fast becoming the world's fintech capital, despite having substantially fewer resources available for investment than the US.

Next summer Copenhagen will host Money 20/20, the world's major annual event for emerging payment technology. It will be the first time the forum convenes outside the US, bearing witness to the increasing importance of Europe when it comes to innovation in payments and financial technology. In countries like The Netherlands there are cafes and even supermarkets that no longer accept cash.

Many have pointed to the slow death of cash in Scandinavia, but cash is unlikely to completely die out – few may develop a mobile app suited to the needs of refugee migrants there, for example.

North America

Despite playing host to the world's top technology firms and research centres, the US lags behind when it comes to implementing some of this tech. Chip and pin payment cards were only launched in October 2015 and do not seem to have done well over the Christmas holiday season, with reports of large retailers bypassing card readers and going back to signatures. This might seem backward but it's important to remember that chip and pin cards are as much a protocol to determine who will bear the cost of fraud as a security feature.

And, while the US has been slow to introduce chip and pin, there have been developments in smartphone payments. The bank JP Morgan Chase and retailer Walmart have both launched rivals to Apple Pay, which shows how retailers, banks and regulators are innovating to bring about faster payments and a potential cashless society.

Africa and the Middle East

The success of the mobile payments system, M-Pesa, in increasing financial inclusion in Kenya is well known, with the majority of the population able to transfer money using their phones, despite not having a bank account. And there has been similar growth of mobile payments in Botswana and South Africa. But Safaricom (the telecom company behind M-Pesa) has failed to replicate its model in neighbouring countries such as Tanzania. The jury is also out regarding the Cash-less Nigeria Project by its central bank, which aims to reduce the amount of physical cash circulating in the economy.

Africa and the Middle East remain the areas with the lowest global numbers of adults with a bank account while MENA countries (as well as China and other Asia-Pacific nations) have been and will continue to be the world's growth markets for ATM manufacturers. This suggests the high use of banknotes in the everyday life of people in these regions.

Asia, Latin America and Oceania

In China, the mobile app WeChat is one to watch. WeChat, part of digital behemoth Tencent, has grown from its original service as a messaging app in 2011 to include cab-hailing, food-ordering and money transfers. WeChat ranks as China's most popular app with 650m users and is used to send both RMB and cryptocurrencies like bitcoin between users.

Technology as a promoter of financial inclusion is the name of the game in poor economies where the bottom third of the population hardly have any access to the financial sector and mobile money is seen as the potential solution. Chile is a notable example of successful government initiatives in this direction. But the one to watch is the Indian Government's drive to replace money with mobile payments on top of a growing private network made up of 140,000 private business and public sector bank correspondents.

The challenge for mobile money, however, is that it sits at the intersection of finance and telecommunication and so faces regulations from both. On top of that, India and other countries in Asia and Latin America have a significant number of transactions that take place outside the formal financial sector and typically, an over-regulated telecommunications sector. At the same time, those at the 'bottom of the pyramid' are fearful of and distrust established financial institutions.

Australia offers a much brighter outlook. The introduction of contactless payment cards in 2010 has proven hugely successful and as a result plastic has significantly eroded the use of cash and ATMs. Indeed, a recent study by the Reserve Bank of Australia found that the use of banknotes and coins fell from 69% in 2007 to just 47% in 2013. That decline took place across all age and income groups, with people in rural locations more likely to be using cash than those in major cities.

While some countries have embraced mostly electronic forms of payment, this does not mean that others still using banknotes and coins are less efficient or backward as some might seem to think. Differences between countries and between rich and poor within them remain partly due to custom, culture and regulation. But also because new technology has failed to make its case to users.

There is more innovative technology looking for a market than consumers looking for alternative ways to pay. And there is nothing wrong with existing forms of payment – they, and cash in particular, work well in most countries, for most consumers, 99% of the time. Of course, people change their habits and financial technology start-ups may one day disrupt the status quo.

8 January 2017

⇨   The above information is reprinted with kind permission from *The Conversation*. Please visit www.theconversation.co.uk for further information.

© 2017 The Conversation Trust (UK)

Britons ditching cheques and paying bills by contactless card, figures show

Britons are now more likely to pay by contactless card than with a cheque, new quarterly figures show.

Less than a third of Britons (31%) have used cheques in the past three months, down from 40% who used them to make a payment in 2015, analysts Mintel said.

Cheques are now the least likely method British shoppers choose to pay with, behind contactless debit cards (39%) and contactless credit cards (34%).

Just 28% of consumers used a contactless debit card to make a payment last year, but this has grown to 39%, while the use of contactless credit cards has increased from 28% last year to 34%.

However, 54% of consumers are not comfortable with the potential for a completely cashless society.

Almost all Britons (97%) used cash in the three months to April, making this the most common payment method.

Mintel financial services analyst Rich Shepherd said: "Part of the reason for the rapid increase in the use of contactless cards is the simple fact that they are now much more widely accepted. They've moved beyond coffee shops and sandwich bars and are now entirely commonplace.

"However, the real shift in behaviour has only come over the last few years. It's easy to forget that contactless cards were first launched back in 2007, meaning that the technology has been on British high streets for almost a decade.

"People's payment habits change slowly, as can be seen with the cheque's stubborn refusal to disappear from the payments landscape."

9 May 2017

⇨   The above information is reprinted with kind permission from the Press Association. Please visit www.pressassociation.com for further information.

© 2017 Press Association

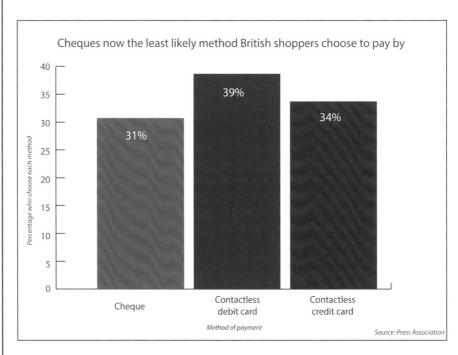

Cheques now the least likely method British shoppers choose to pay by

Source: Press Association

Tap-and-go fraud warning: cards can be used AFTER you cancel them

By Katie Morley, Consumer Affairs Editor

Contactless cardholders who cancel their cards after having them stolen are still at risk of fraud, it has emerged, as the process does not always stop them being used by thieves in shops.

An investigation by consumer website moneysavingexpert. com discovered cancelled cards being used up to eight months later by criminals to buy items in shops.

People whose contactless cards have been lost or stolen are being told to comb through months or years' worth of statements to check for fraudulent transactions which may not have been flagged by their bank.

The problem is borne from a tap-and-go technology loophole which lets thieves make so-called "offline" payments without the bank which issued the card being informed.

"Contactless card use has grown rapidly in recent years as a handy alternative to cash. A year ago, the contactless card limit for a single transaction was raised by £10, to £30"

The only way to detect such payments is by going through people's bank statements.

Offline payments are stored in batches by retailers and processed online to the bank at a later point, sometimes a few days later with smaller stores. This can allow a thief buying goods on a stolen card to go unnoticed.

Other payments – often in larger stores – are processed online which means the card and payment machine immediately communicate with the customer's bank.

If a lost or stolen card has been cancelled, this will be flagged immediately and a payment not allowed. Fraud on contactless cards is rare and considerably lower than overall card fraud.

As a safety measure some firms set a 'floor limit' at which payments are forced to go online – meaning anything above a certain amount is checked out immediately with the issuing bank.

The report from moneysavingexpert. com said the "chaotic system" means that while some accounts are prevented from being raided by this type of fraud, in other cases it is left to customers to spot dodgy payments.

In March, contactless card spending in the UK topped £1.5 billion in the space of a month for the first time.

A spokesman for the UK Cards Association said: "Fraud on contactless cards is rare and considerably lower than overall card fraud. Consumers are fully protected against any fraud losses and will not be left out of pocket.

"As always it is important to check bank or card statements regularly for any unusual transactions, especially if a card has been lost or stolen. When a customer reports a lost or stolen card they will be advised to report any transactions they do not recognise to their bank."

27 July 2017

⇨ The above information is reprinted with kind permission from *The Telegraph*. Please visit www. thetelegraph.co.uk for further information.

© Telegraph Media Group Limited 2017

One in three would be more likely to donate to charity if they could use contactless payment

By Stephen Harmston

The lack of contactless options for charitable donors is hampering giving, a new YouGov study suggests.

"The 'Charitable Giving 2017' report indicates that one in three (30%) of Britons would be more likely to donate to charity in some way if they could do so by using contactless technology"

The research highlights the broad range of donation types that contactless could open up. One in ten (11%) would be more likely to donate using contactless when giving a one-off payment to someone collecting cash for charity in the street (i.e. a collection box).

This is closely followed by the 9% that would be more likely to buy something being sold for charity on the street (i.e. *The Big Issue*). Some 7% say they would give a one-off payment to a street fundraiser while 6% said they would be more likely to donate by tapping on a poster or advert in newspaper or magazine. Perhaps unsurprisingly, those in the younger age groups would be most likely to consider charitable contactless donation with over half (52%) of 18-34s saying this option would make them more likely to donate. This compares to three in ten (30%) 35-54 year-olds and one in seven (16%) over-55s. In fact, one in five (20%) 18-34 year-olds would be more likely to give one-off payments to those collecting if they could use their card.

'Almost half (48%) of those who are likely to donate by contactless believe it would be more convenient while a third (33%) think that by giving in this way they would know that cash wasn't being misspent. Furthermore, a third (32%) want contactless options because they either don't carry cash at all or carry enough cash that they can donate.'

Contactless payment has transformed transactions across many industries, especially retail and transport where consumers and businesses are looking for speed and ease. On-street donations fit a similar pattern where many people are in a rush and, while they want to give, they want to do it quickly. Our report indicates that there is public appetite for this form of donation, and if charities can help alleviate some barriers to giving that people currently face the rewards could be great.

7 March 2017

⇨ The above information is reprinted with kind permission from YouGov. Please visit www. yougov.co.uk for further information.

© 2017 YouGov plc

The rise of cryptocurrencies

Not since when I remember PayPal appearing on the scene way back in the late 90s can I remember a time when 'digital currency' was everywhere I looked online.

The ability to have a currency that isn't tied to either the Government or your local or national Bank is quite a unique one still and one that can take quite some time to get your head around when you first get exposed to it.

The latest version is what are called cryptocurrencies, which is a blanket term for all digital exchanges that take place and include some kind of cryptography framework around them and the necessary security features.

Things are getting so big in the world of cryptocurrencies that even the PM of Malta is saying they should be embraced.

Cryptocurrencies started in 2009 when bitcoin became the first decentralized cryptocurrency

One of the major benefits of digital currency is the community that is build around it. When an Olympian from India wasn't convinced he could afford the $5,000 needed to attend the 2014 Winter Olympics in Russia a section of Reddit raised the money in a couple of hours through the use of Dogecoin.

bitcoin (probably the most well known digital currency out there) is currently enjoying record levels and was valued at $1,025USD at the beginning of this year (and has actually risen since!). Indeed many have said that one of the reasons that bitcoin has been flourishing is because of the uncertainty of Donald Trump and the Brexit vote last year.

If you do any kind of online earning it's only a matter of time before you get exposed to people proposing that you can make money via cryptocurrencies such as bitcoin but what different ways are there to actually earn money when you get involved in them.

There are really three main ways you can make money from cryptocurrencies:

Mining

Here you can use your computer's processing power to literally mine for electronic currency. In the past you were able to do this using your regular home laptop but now you tend to need quite a high spec machine that is able to deal with the maths calculations at the speed needed to actually mine any coins to benefit. Otherwise all you are doing is spending more on your electricity bill than you are making electronic currency!

Spectate

Just as buying stocks and shares it's all about GETTING IN EARLY. There are a lot of alt coins out there such as Peercoin and Novacoin. So it's about taking your time to get some good knowledge in the industry and looking to buy when they are at their cheapest and then waiting maybe 6–12 months until they have matured enough to make you a good profit when you sell them on.

Trading

This is without doubt the easiest way to make money from cryptocurrencies and where big time players like Jay Edward Smith have made their money on the trading platform eToro. You can start with as little or as much money as you want and can of course always cash out at any time you want. I should warn you though that the market can show a LOT of VOLATILITY which is why you can make so much money from it if you get your timings right and trade the right currencies.

If you did want to give trading a go then I would recommend you do look at using a platform such as eToro. It is very simple to use and understand. It has over six million users from all around the world and the site has a real emphasis on the social side of trading which makes it a better experience for everyone involved.

Whichever way you decide to go when it comes to electronic currencies always make sure you do your research before investing in anything of this nature.

27 March 2017

⇨ The above information is reprinted with kind permission from The Money Shed Blog. Please visit www.blog.themoneyshed.co.uk for further information.

A bit of change: Indians using bitcoin to trade, shop, even pay for pizza

By Rachel Lopez

There are now one million bitcoin enthusiasts in the country, ranging from a Delhi housewife to a Mumbai undertaker and a trader from Gujarat.

Vishal Gupta's ears ring with the sound of coins he can't touch. The 34-year-entrepreneur was gifted a single bitcoin, then worth a mere Rs 3,100, back in 2011 and it got him hooked on to the idea of virtual money. Today, one bitcoin is worth close to Rs 40,000 and Gupta is waiting for India to realise that the currency is valuable not just in itself, but also for what it's starting to represent.

It's been around only since 2009. It circulates only as strings of code through a network of servers across the world. But Gupta believes bitcoin is the ideal monetary system for our connected, wired, post-recession world. "Cash is unwieldy and unsafe. Cheques and credit cards need banks," he points out. "But banks are incentivised to take risks, so they keep making a mess and get bailed out at the literal cost of the people."

bitcoin is different. "It is operated by the very people who use it, so it offers the accountability and trust that our banks cannot," he says. "It also has no geographical boundaries. Unlike a dollar, a dirham or a rupee, a bitcoin has the same value the world over." The idea excited Gupta so much, he gave up his in-cab advertising business two years ago and set up SearchTrade, a company that collaborates with search engines. He pays his contributors in bitcoin.

Over the last few years, bitcoin's reputation has cleaned up like a shiny new penny. Headlines have gone from alarmist (the 2013 bust of drug-trade site Silk Road, which accepted the currency) to awestruck (hackers stealing $65 million worth of bitcoins in a single heist in August). Governments, lawmakers, bankers and investors have begun studying it closely. Enterprises as varied as MobiKwik, Dell, Expedia, Virgin Galactic and Wikileaks now accept it as payment. In India, bitcoin enthusiasts now number one million. They include everyone from geeks to granddads, in big cities and little towns. They encompass brokers and businessmen, lawyers and homemakers, spenders and hoarders, hackers and the hacked. Here are some of them.

The virtual spender

Monisha Kalra learnt about the currency from her son, Mohit, and turned her kitty party gang into bitcoin users.

Kalra knew that trading in bitcoin could be rewarding. What she hadn't anticipated was her gang of 40 kitty party friends becoming interested in it too. "The difficult part was to explain how bitcoins were generated, because even I didn't understand it well," she said. But with help from her son, web videos, and multiple discussions, "my friends got curious about investing a little money to start with".

Kalra has used her bitcoin earnings to shop on e-stores. "I was excited to spend bitcoin for the first time and was amazed at how easy it is to use," she says. "It's as simple as using payTM or Mobiquik." The unexpected bonus: "My friends have started calling me the bitcoin Mom."

The miner

Mumbai undertaker Danny Pinto is among those who can seemingly generate bitcoins from thin air.

Pinto, 59, had been a marine engineer and a transport entrepreneur before he set up a successful chain of funeral parlours. "I'm always on the lookout for something new," he says. So when he heard of bitcoin from a friend in November, he was intrigued by the idea of mining – being rewarded in bitcoins for running the currency's ledger or global accounting system.

Mining, he found out, is rewarding but competitive work. Miners jointly buy servers in countries with cheap electricity, uninterrupted internet and frigid temperatures to keep machines cool, and then they split the bitcoin reward. "It takes a few days to figure out. But once people realise it's the computers doing all the work, they stop being intimidated." He signed on in December with his first bitcoin, then worth Rs 22,000.

"Since then, I've put all my investments into mining," he says, claiming he gets 9% returns every month. Pinto is trying to convince his son to accept bitcoin payments in their undertakers' business. "It's the money of the future. And it can be your last payment before you go!"

The simplifier

In Ahmedabad, Sandeep Goenka's start-up is helping make bitcoin as easy to use as cash.

Angel investor Goenka realised Bitcoin's potential back in 2013. He also knew that its complicated functioning would put off most users. "I didn't want to be a Chief Explaining Officer," he says. "I wanted bitcoin to be as simple to use as WhatsApp." His solution: joining up with enthusiasts Saurabh Agrawal and Mahin Gupta to form ZebPay. The app lets smartphone users buy and sell bitcoins. It also lets them spend bitcoin to pay their cellphone and DTH cable TV bills, buy data and talktime top-ups and etailing and pizza vouchers, just like they'd spend regular money.

The 13-month-old company's trade turnover was 18,700 bitcoins or about Rs 75 crore last month. Their app crossed 1 lakh downloads across Android and iOS, last month. Goenka's own bitcoin wealth, made by incremental investments over the last year, now has, "a 150% increase in value," he says. "I've never sold; I think the price will rise higher."

The early adopter

For Delhi entrepreneur Mohit Kalra, bitcoin is the curious gamble that's starting to pay off.

If, at 24, Kalra, is already the CEO of a bitcoin company, it's only because he

Cracking the code: what is bitcoin, how does it work?

So how does virtual currency run, with neither banks nor borders?
With a little help from maths, technology, and a community of enthusiasts.

Invented in 2008 by an anonymous person or group that goes by the name Satoshi Makamoto bitcoin is a currency that exists only as lines of code.

Users exchange regular currency to buy bitcoins, which are stored in a wallet or digital account.

All accounts need PAN card verification in India. Most other countries ask for government, issued photo-identification.

Only 21 million bitcoins have been created by Nakamotos, 15.2 million are in circulation and new ones are released (or mined) slowly to protect value.

One bitcoin is worth Rs 40,000 today but you can split each bitcoin into 10crore satoshis (each worth less than a third of a paisa today), so there's enough to go around, save or spend.

Each bitcoin has its own unique code and is created via a process called mining.

This process is part game, part race and part lottery. Shared servers race to solve billions of calculations per second and winners – called miners – get rewarded in bitcoins.

Every time a unit of a bitcoin is used, the same servers around the world take note, recording the transaction in a public ledger for the record, preventing double-spending.

Like regular money, bitcoins get circulated when you use them – to buy e-vouchers, spend on vacation, pay phone or cable TV bills, transfer money internationally, or just to order a pizza.

bitcoin lets you spend your digital money securely, keeping your identity private even though the transaction itself is publicly verified.

This means you can transfer currency across the world or back home without going to a bank. The money is transferred in minutes, without middlemen, leaks or bank transfer fees, which can be as high as 30%.

started early. Kalra's interest in financial technologies as a student led him to mine bitcoin "just for the experience" in 2010, when a bitcoin was worth less than a dollar. By 2013, when it crossed $260, he was still among India's largest miners. "I had all these coins but no way to spend them," Kalra says.

This prompted him to set up Coinsecure, the first website that let Indians buy and sell bitcoins smoothly in rupees, with fellow enthusiast Benson Samuel. Today, users can start with as little as Rs 100 worth of bitcoin, practise on a mock platform before trading, and cash out through reputed banks.

"We trade about 9,000 bitcoins a month," Kalra claims. About 15% of the users are women, many of them over 30, and "a good number are students who need bitcoin because they can't use debit cards on foreign sites".

bitcoin is finally getting India interested, Kalra says. "Even a year ago, when I told people my job, they'd assume I was doing something shady, like selling drugs, or running a hawala scam," he says. "These days, they want to know how and how quickly they can start using it."

The unwilling recruit

Delhi businessman Abhishek adopted bitcoin the hard way, when hackers demanded a ransom in the virtual currency.

In July, Abhishek (last name withheld on request) walked into his Delhi office to find all his computers jammed, his banking details compromised and a few key files encrypted. "My screen just showed a five-day deadline counting down, and a message to transfer something called 'satoshis' to a specified account number." He'd been hacked, and the hackers had set a ransom of 17,000 satoshis (10 million satoshis make up 1 bitcoin), worth about Rs 8,000 at the time. Delhi's Cyber Crime cell couldn't help. But, in two days, Abhishek set up a bitcoin account, bought the satoshis and transferred them to the hackers.

"I cut my internet wire the second I recovered my data," he recalls. "It taught me a few things – that I need to keep my data more secure. But that the bitcoin system itself is clean."

The broker

In Jaipur, Shubham Nawariya sees bitcoin's volatile price as the perfect opportunity for profit.

Nawariya, a 22-year-old computer science graduate, discovered bitcoin a year ago, watching friends shop from international sites without paying bank fees. "It was confusing – how do you count something that doesn't exist?" he says. But by the time he took his final exams in April, he'd learned enough to trade bitcoins online like stocks and help people transfer money between India and the world.

He now trades full-time, going through about 3 bitcoins (Rs 1.16 lakh) every day. "I have to keep explaining to people that, in India, no one is interested in buying drugs with bitcoin," he says, laughing. "It's for sending money anywhere, in a few minutes, with no leaks, instead of running around between banks the whole day. And, of course, to stash your wealth."

15 February 2017

⇨ The above information is reprinted with kind permission from *Hindustan Times*. Please visit www.hindustantimes.com for further information.

© 2017 Hindustan Times

Mastercard app lets online shoppers pay with a selfie

MasterCard is launching its Identity Check Mobile technology in 12 countries.

By Zlata Rodionova

Mastercard has confirmed that it is to start accepting "selfies" and fingerprint recognition as an alternative to passwords when verifying IDs for online payments.

The US card company has rolled out the technology in the UK and 11 other European countries including Spain, Germany and Finland.

To access the new function, customers must download the new Identity Check Mobile app, through which they can authorise payment with a fingerprint or face recognition.

The service requires users to take a selfie with their mobile device and upload their photo to Mastercard, which then creates a digital map of their face, ready to be used when a purchase needs to be verified.

The credit card firm has been testing selfie software in the US, Canada and

12 countries are now trying 'pay with a selfie' technology

83% of people who tested the new technology said it was more secure than passwords

Netherlands. Some 92 per cent of test subjects preferred the new system to passwords.

Some security researchers have said that biometric checks have the potential to cut fraud, but others have warned that they might not be as secure as traditional methods.

Of those who tested the software, 83 per cent said it was more secure than passwords.

Ajay Bhalla, president, enterprise risk and security, Mastercard, said the initiative is a "significant milestone" in the evolution of payments.

"Shopping in person has been revolutionized thanks to advances like contactless cards, mobile payments and wearables, and now we are making Identity Check Mobile a reality for online shopping in Europe, and soon, the world," he said.

27 July 2017

⇨ The above information is reprinted with kind permission from *The Independent*. Please visit www.independent.co.uk for further information.

How getting rid of 'black money' has driven a digital treasure hunt in India

An article from The Conversation.

By Yogesh K Dwivedi, Personal Chair and Director of Research, Swansea University; Kuttimani Tamilmani, PhD Researcher, Swansea University and Nripendra Rana, Associate Professor of Information Systems, Swansea University

In what can only be described as a historic opportunity to weed out evils in the country's shadow economy, the Indian prime minister, Narendra Modi, has announced that all 500 and 1,000 rupee notes have been stripped of their status as legal tender, as his party intensifies its strike on "black money".

The two notes make up about 86% of the currency in circulation by value in India and represent the maximum – and most popular – currency denominations. Their demonetisation has been both praised and criticised in the international media – and the people of India themselves are equally split.

So why demonetise the notes? India's Ministry of Finance has said that the purpose is to curb financing of terrorism and any other subversive activities through the proceeds of fake currency notes. It also aims to restrain the shadow economy in India, the major driver of inflation that adversely affects the poor and deprives the government of its tax revenues. In addition, it is hoped that the move will reduce cash circulation in the country – as most corrupt activities and illegal dealings are done through cash.

The move is also expected to unearth people's real income and ensure those falling under certain brackets pay taxes promptly. At present just 1% of the country's people are paying income tax.

Cashing out

In the West, many would likely think that the revocation of certain bank notes, though it may cause some inconvenience, would be no problem. After all, the large majority have bank accounts and debit and credit cards to use. But in India it is a different story – banking is still considered to be a luxury for the majority of people who are below the poverty line. Despite current government attempts to ensure financial inclusion, many still use only notes and coins to pay for goods and services. In fact, it is estimated that 95% of transactions in India are made using cash and, for those squirrelling money away, it is a necessity to survive.

Though the announcement came as a surprise to some sectors of the public (and many politicians), the ruling party has been determined to eradicate black money from the moment it took power. A special investigations team was set up in 2014 to curb the menace of black money – and the screws of justice have been gradually tightened through the amendment of a series of measures such as the double taxation avoidance agreements.

The people of India have been given until the end of business hours on December 30, 2016 to exchange or deposit their notes in banks and post offices. Other measures have also been put in place to make sure that the procedure runs smoothly and is as convenient as possible for the public.

Social help

Though its intentions for the country's economy appear positive, the move has not been well received by the common man. Tempers are flaring and some are warning of riots over the abrupt change. The poor, who are unused to dealing with banks, have mainly been left by authorities to wait in long queues outside financial institutions simply to figure out what to do with their notes.

Social media has been flooded with rumours – and conspiracy theories abound. They include the notion that the new 2,000 Rupee note has an embedded electronic chip. But volunteers are also using social media sites to make sure that no one loses out and are crowd-sourcing and sharing information on what to do and where to go.

Digital banking companies have also risen to the challenge, setting up shop in more convenient places to allow people to sign up and use their money as they wish. Paytm, an e-wallet firm, has seen a huge surge in transactions, for example – even a roadside stall has started to accept payments through e-wallet.

The removal of the notes has also brought India's first "digital and cashless village", Akodara, which is 60 miles from the northern city of Ahmedabad, into the limelight. Most of the 1,200 people living in Akodara buy everything from wheat flour to potato chips through mobile banking and have little to worry about when it comes to the demonetisation.

The Reserve Bank of India has also been encouraging citizens to make use of internet and mobile banking at least in the short term as it works to "alleviate the pressure on the physical currency".

True though it may be that demonetisation has brought with it an inevitable slowdown, the act could be the start of a new economy for India. One that is far more inclusive, and helps to educate the people of India on the benefits of transactions in a digital world.

18 November 2016

⇨ The above information is reprinted with kind permission from *The Conversation*. Please visit www.theconversation.com for further information.

Android Pay UK app launches as rival to Apple Pay and Samsung Pay

By Thomas Tamblyn

The Android Pay app is now live in the UK, giving Android users the ability to pay using their smartphones.

Android Pay can be used at any wireless payment point so if it supports your contactless card or Apple Pay then you're good to go with Android Pay.

Google's new contactless payment service joins an increasing number of apps and services including Samsung Pay and PayPal which are trying to encourage people to move away from using their conventional bank cards as a means of paying. How Do I Get Android Pay?

Android Pay is only compatible with Android smartphones that are running Android 4.4+ AND are equipped with NFC.

Recently released Android smartphones should come with Android Pay pre-installed but if you think you're missing out you can always head over to the Google Play Store and download the app separately from there.

Which UK banks support Android Pay?

Much like Apple Pay, there's good news and bad news concerning the banks. While many of the big players are in there it's hard not to notice the glaring omission that is Barclays.

⇨ Bank of Scotland

⇨ first direct

⇨ Halifax

⇨ HSBC

⇨ Lloyds

⇨ M&S Bank

⇨ MBNA

⇨ Nationwide

How do i add my card to Android Pay?

There are two ways to add a payment card:

On your phone

⇨ Open the Android Pay app.

⇨ If you have multiple Google Accounts in Android Pay: At the top left of the app, touch your name, then choose the account you want to add a card to.

⇨ At the bottom right, touch the plus sign +.

⇨ Touch Add a credit or debit card.

⇨ Use the camera to capture your card info or enter it manually.

⇨ **On the web**

⇨ Sign in to payments.google.com.

⇨ On the left, click Payment methods.

⇨ At the top, click Add a payment method > Add a card.

⇨ Enter your card info, then click Save

How secure is Android Pay?

Android Pay secures your bank details in slightly different way to Apply Pay.

Whereas on Apple's devices the details are stored in a 'vault' on the phone, Google chooses to keep your payment details securely stored on their cloud servers.

While both are equally secure not all Android phones have this hardware advantage that Apple's products do so Google had to find an alternative solution.

Either way your bank details are never permanently kept on your Android phone so if it's ever lost or stolen (or hacked) they won't be visible.

Whenever a purchase is made, a virtual account number is then sent to the payment terminal instead of your payment details.

18 May 2016

⇨ The above information is reprinted with kind permission from The Huffington Post UK. Please visit www.huffingtonpost.co.uk for further information.

Key facts

⇨ Average weekly household spending remained level at £528.90 in the financial year ending 2016, coinciding with a slowdown in consumer confidence. (page 1)

⇨ Low-income households continued to spend a higher proportion of their expenditure on food and energy when compared with households with a higher income. (page 1)

⇨ UK households spent more than £45.00 a week on restaurants and hotels for the first time in five years. (page 1)

⇨ Average weekly spending on alcohol, tobacco and narcotics fell below £12.00 for the first time. (page 1)

⇨ Over half of money spent on communication was spent on a mobile phone-related cost. (page 1)

⇨ Total average weekly household expenditure remained level at £528.90 in the financial year ending 2016 (2015/16) when compared with the same period a year ago. (page 2)

⇨ A full-time nursery place for a child under two costs an eye-watering £222 a week, meaning working families are now spending £11,300 a year on average on childcare. This increases to £15,700 in London. (page 2)

⇨ Research from Legal & General and Cebr showed that parents will be involved in 26% of all property transactions in 2017, contributing towards more than 298,000 mortgages and helping to purchase homes worth £75 billion. (page 3)

⇨ Almost two-thirds (63%) of parents expect pocket money to be spent on sweets and chocolate, however, half (49%) expect their children to buy DVDs and CDs with their pocket money, 45% expect tickets (for the cinema, theatre or concert) to be bought and 44% expect their children to buy video games. (page 4)

⇨ Factors that influence how much pocket money parents give to their children are:

 • The cost of items their children want (39%)

 • Recent behaviour (37%)

 • School grades (30%). (page 4)

⇨ Children under the age of five receive £2 a week pocket money in the UK, compared with 80p in Spain, 40p in The Netherlands and £1.60 in France. The Italians are more indulgent, at £4. (page 5)

⇨ Brits save an average £150 each month – a collective £81.8 billion a year. (page 10)

⇨ But a fifth have no savings at all and 18 per cent save £50 or less. (page 10)

⇨ 53% wish they had received more money advice at a younger age as 78% believe being "good with money" is a learned behaviour. (page 10)

⇨ According to a recent study:

 • Around four out of ten adults are not in control of their finances

 • One in five cannot read a bank statement

 • Four in ten adults have less than £500 in savings

 • One in three cannot calculate the impact of a 2% annual interest rate on £100 in savings. (page 15)

⇨ In total, 28% of all UK house-holds say they experience some form of financial stress be it relying more on overdrafts and loans or struggling to pay bills. (page 17)

⇨ Total unsecured debt for UK households (which includes credit cards, payday loans etc and student loans. but not mortgages) rose by £48bn between 2012 and 2015 to reach £353bn. Unsecured debt previously peaked at £364bn in 2008 and fell in the recession. The increase since 2012 increase is in part due to the major extension of student loans. (page 18)

⇨ Households in problem debt have to spend more than 25 per cent of their monthly income paying the interest on their debts (credit cards, loans, overdrafts, arrears). (page 19)

⇨ In addition to unsecured credit commitments, four in ten people are behind on their household bills. This is an increase of 5% over the last five years. On top of their unsecured debts, this amounts to an additional average debt burden of £2,061 for these clients. (page 21)

⇨ There are 13 million people in the UK who do not have enough savings to support them for one month if they experienced a 25% cut in income. (page 23)

⇨ Cheques are now the least likely method British shoppers choose to pay with, behind contactless debit cards (39%) and contactless credit cards (34%). (page 31)

⇨ Contactless card use has grown rapidly in recent years as a handy alternative to cash. A year ago, the contactless card limit for a single transaction was raised by £10, to £30

Bursary

An amount of money given to a student by the college or university to attend. It does not have to be paid back.

Credit card

A card that is issued, usually by a bank or business, for purchasing goods or services on 'credit'. 'Credit' is essentially a promise to pay for something later – this is then paid back. While the debt remains unpaid, it will continue to increase with interest until it is paid off in full.

Debt

Something, usually money, that is owed and needs to be repaid.

Household income

The combined amount of money earned by all members of a household.

Interest

A charge that is added while a debt continues to be owed.

Loan

An amount of money that is borrowed and is expected to be paid back, usually with interest.

Maintenance grant/loan

An amount of money given to students from the Government to help pay for their living expenses while they study. A maintenance loan has to be paid back; a maintenance grant does not.

Overdraft

Money that is withdrawn from a bank account and causes the balance to fall below zero.

Redundancy

An amount of money paid by an employer when there is no longer the need or capacity for you to remain employed by them.

Retirement

The time in a person's life when they stop work completely.

Scholarship

An amount of money paid to a student to attend a university or college, usually on the basis of academic or sporting achievement. Does not have to be repaid.

State Pension

An amount of money provided by the Government upon retirement.

Student loan

A sum of money lent to students by the Government in order to pay for their tuition and maintenance fees. Is paid back gradually once the graduate is earning over £21,000 per year.

Tuition fees

The amount of money charged by a university or college for the course of study they are providing.

Assignments

Brainstorming

⇨ In small groups, discuss what you know about banking.

- What is banking?

- What is the difference between a debit and credit card?

- What are contactless payments?

- What does the term 'paying with a selfie' mean?

Research

⇨ Ask your parents about their monthly outgoings. Create a graph showing their monthly spend. e.g. how much are their utiLity bills? How much do they spend on entertainment per month? How much does it cost to run their car?

⇨ Research Bitcoins and how they can be used. List the pros and cons of using this type of currency.

⇨ Talk to your friends and family and see how many of them use contactless payments. Take into consideration other types of payments used by people of different ages and gender. Write a summary of your findings and include a graph to illustrate the different payments methods used by the different groups.

⇨ Research 'Financial Inclusion'. What does this term mean? How does being excluded from this affect people? Write a report no longer than two pages long.

⇨ Ask your classmates how much pocket money they receive. Take into account whether they have to do jobs in order to receive it or whether this money is just given to them. How often do they receive pocket money? Is it weekly or monthly? Is there a difference between what the boys and girls in your class receive? Produce an infographic to show your findings.

Design

⇨ In pairs design your own bitcoin.

⇨ Produce a leaflet informing people about debt, its causes and suggest ways to get help and to deal with the problem.

⇨ Design a poster which will encourage shoppers to pay using a 'mobile selfie'.

⇨ Choose an article from the book and design your own illustration highlighting its key points.

⇨ Design your own bank. It should include all the latest technology for people to use. Make it a bright, fun place to visit.

Oral

⇨ Have a class discussion about the latest payment technology available which can be used by shoppers both online and instore.

⇨ In pairs go through this book and discuss the cartoons you come across. Think about what the artists were trying to portray with each illustration.

⇨ In small groups discuss the demise of cash in the UK. What is taking its place? Make a note of your discussion and share it with the rest of the class.

⇨ In pairs create a presentation encouraging older people to use contactless payments. You should point out the benefits as well as the risks.

Reading/writing

⇨ Read the article *Students struggling under debt-stress while at university* on page 26 and draw an illustration that highlights the key points of the article.

⇨ Imagine you are an Agony Aunt/Uncle writing for a magazine. You have received a letter from a female student who is struggling with debt and thinking of leaving university. Write a reply advising her where to go for help and support.

⇨ Write a summary of the article *A bit of change: Indians using bitcoin to trade, shop, even pay for pizza* on page 35.

⇨ Write a blog post about the 'Bank of Mum and Dad' from the point of view that you are the recipient. Explain how your parents have helped you financially and what the money went towards.

⇨ Write a definition of 'a cashless economy'

⇨ Write a paragraph about tap-and-go fraud.

⇨ A friend has written to you and asked you about cryptocurrencies and if you think they are a good idea. Write a letter back from either one of these two points of view:

- You do agree with the use of them and explain why

- You do not agree with the use of them and explain why.

⇨ Write an article about payday loans. Explain how these work and how they can lead to debt. Advise people of any other options they could use instead.

Acknowledgements

The publisher is grateful for permission to reproduce the material in this book. While every care has been taken to trace and acknowledge copyright, the publisher tenders its apology for any accidental infringement or where copyright has proved untraceable. The publisher would be pleased to come to a suitable arrangement in any such case with the rightful owner.

Images

All images courtesy of iStock except pages 3, 8, 22, 29, 34 and 37: Pixabay, page 28 © Mobilepayment and page 33 © Courtney hedger

Icons

Icons on pages 5, 11 and 12 were made by Freepik from www.flaticon.com. Icon on page 13 was made by RoundIcon from www.flaticon.com.

Illustrations

Don Hatcher: pages 4 & 17. Simon Kneebone: pages 1 & 6.

Additional acknowledgements

Editorial on behalf of Independence Educational Publishers by Cara Acred.

With thanks to the Independence team: Shelley Baldry, Tina Brand, Sandra Dennis, Jackie Staines and Jan Sunderland.

Cara Acred

Cambridge, September 2017